POWERFUL ELEMENT OF A GREAT NATION

"Pillars of Progress: The Dynamic Forces Propelling a Great Nation Towards Eminence" all nations need these Elements to be Great in this 21st Century.

ANDREW BEATTIE

TABLE OF CONTENTS

INTRODUCTION

In the annals of human history, the saga of Great Nations unfurls like an epic narrative, replete with triumphs and tribulations, conquests and collapses. Yet, amidst the tumultuous currents of geopolitics and the ever-shifting tides of fortune, one singular element emerges as the linchpin of national greatness: the indomitable spirit of its populace. Beyond the confines of geographical boundaries and the ephemeral glories of wealth and power, it is the collective will, intellect, and resilience of a nation's people that form the bedrock of its ascendancy to eminence.

Consider the ancient civilizations of Greece, where the citadel of Athens burgeoned into a beacon of enlightenment, casting its radiance across the known world. Here, amidst the marble columns and bustling agora, it was not the mere expanse of territory or the opulence of its treasury that secured Athens' stature, but rather the intellectual ferment of its citizens. From the profound ruminations of philosophers like Socrates and Plato to the artistic splendor epitomized by the Parthenon, the essence of Athenian greatness lay in the fertile soil of human creativity and discourse.

Similarly, cast your gaze upon the mist-shrouded shores of Britannia during the throes of the industrial revolution. As the clangor of machinery reverberated through the valleys and chimneys pierced the heavens, it was not merely the abundance of coal or the strategic prowess of the British Empire that propelled it to the zenith of global influence. Rather, it was the ingenuity, perseverance, and toil of countless men and women, laboring in the foundries and textile mills, that forged the sinews of Britain's economic might.

In the crucible of modernity, the United States emerged as a crucible of democratic fervor, a testament to the enduring power of a nation conceived in liberty and dedicated to the proposition that all men are created equal. Here, against the backdrop of a vast continent, it was not the expanses of fertile plains or the bounty of natural resources alone that underpinned America's rise to preeminence. Instead, it was the collective aspirations of its citizenry, enshrined in the hallowed words of the Constitution and nurtured through generations of struggle and sacrifice, that propelled the American experiment to unprecedented heights of prosperity and freedom.

Even in the crucible of adversity, amidst the ashes of defeat and devastation, nations have risen phoenix-like from the rubble, their resilience a testament to the indomitable spirit of their people. Consider the post-war renaissance of Japan, where the scars of conflict were transmuted into the crucible of economic miracle through the sweat and toil of a resolute populace, determined to rebuild their nation and reclaim their dignity.

In this grand tapestry of human endeavor, the powerful element of great nations lies not in the caprices of fate or the accidents of geography, but in the boundless potential of their people. It is the capacity for innovation, the resilience in the face of adversity, and the unwavering commitment to shared ideals that distinguish the truly great nations from the ephemeral empires of history. As we embark on this odyssey through the annals of human civilization, let us heed the lessons of the past and celebrate the enduring legacy of the human spirit in shaping the destiny of nations.

CHAPTER 1

LEADERSHIP OF THE NATION

Government leaders are tasked with navigating a complex landscape of priorities that resonate globally. Among these critical objectives are maintaining low inflation rates, reducing unemployment, bolstering the quality of education by ensuring a well-equipped and proficient teaching workforce, and striving for accessible and affordable healthcare systems. Yet, merely listing these priorities barely scratches the surface of the formidable challenges that lie ahead. Achieving these goals demands intricate strategies, collaboration across sectors, and a relentless commitment to effective governance.

Government is a challenging endeavor. Demographics change, budgets fluctuate, and urbanization alters the landscapes of countries, both large and small. Concurrently, the expectations of citizens relentlessly rise. While policymakers highlight numerous achievements, it's evident that many well-intentioned initiatives in governance struggle during implementation. Too frequently, the outcomes fall short of the envisioned goals, resulting in wasted time, resources, and erosion of public trust in leaders and institutions.

It's no surprise, then, that according to the OECD, trust in national governments decreased from 45% to 40% between 2007 and 2012. This decline undermines the willingness of populations to support public institutions through taxation and to engage actively in electoral processes.

AMPLIFYING IMPACT: FOSTERING EFFECTIVE GOVERNANCE

At the heart of governance lies the quest for tangible outcomes—policies that not only articulate noble intentions but also deliver palpable change. Regardless of political landscapes, the essence of governance resonates with citizens' yearning for effective administration. A failure to translate policy rhetoric into substantive action not only breeds disillusionment among the populace but also erects formidable barriers to the implementation of future policy innovations. This imperative has spurred the inception of the Centre for Public Impact by BCG—an altruistic endeavor dedicated to bolstering the transformative potential of governmental initiatives. The journey ahead is expansive and intricate, but the pursuit of impactful governance demands nothing less.

In a sweeping endeavor to gauge the pulse of global governance, the Centre embarked on a comprehensive survey, engaging 1,000 public officials hailing from 25 diverse nations. The resounding consensus echoed a resolute call for heightened implementation efficacy, with a staggering 92% acknowledging ample room for improvement. Digging deeper, nearly half of the respondents confessed to glaring deficiencies in current practices, while a mere 20% claimed consistent utilization of indispensable management tools—such as standardized impact metrics—across their project portfolios. These revelations, though seemingly disparate in origin, converged to underscore a universal truth: the imperative for enhanced impact reverberates across national borders, policy domains, and hierarchical echelons.

In unpacking the anatomy of public impact, the Centre discerned three foundational pillars upon which transformative governance rests: the bedrock of genuine legitimacy, the scaffolding of meticulously crafted policies, and the mortar of effective execution. Yet, the fortification of these pillars necessitates an intricate interplay of ancillary factors—political resolve, operational dexterity, and crystalline objective delineation. Among these, the clarion call for clarity of purpose emerged as a recurring motif, emphasizing the cardinal importance of articulating objectives with precision, charting measurable milestones, and vigilantly monitoring progress along the trajectory of policy implementation.

Embracing this holistic paradigm not only arms policymakers with a potent arsenal to navigate the labyrinth of governance challenges but also empowers them to chart a course towards realizing their policy aspirations with unwavering efficacy. Within the crucible of sustainable economic growth—a cornerstone of societal prosperity and well-being—the confluence of these core elements assumes paramount significance, beckoning policymakers to orchestrate a harmonious symphony of vision, strategy, and execution to unlock the transformative potential of economic policies.

Thomas Hobbes' Leviathan illustrates a world marked by ceaseless insecurity in the absence of government, which is tasked with establishing the safety of law and order. This ensures the protection of citizens from both internal strife and external threats. The dire consequences of lacking such governance are starkly evident in the numerous fragile states and lawless regions globally. In times of heightened chaos and disorder, individuals may even opt for despotic or extremist regimes, like the Taliban or ISIS, viewing them as preferable to the chaos wrought by warring factions.

The concept of government as a protector necessitates the allocation of taxes to finance, train, and equip military and law enforcement entities, construct judicial systems and correctional facilities, and appoint officials to legislate and enforce laws. Concerning external dangers, a protective government must possess the capability to engage diplomatically with other nations and, if necessary, engage in armed conflict. This minimalist governmental perspective mirrors the early structure of the American Republic, comprising the President, Congress, Supreme Court, and key departments such as Treasury, War, State, and Justice.

PROTECT AND PROVIDE

The principle of government serving as both protector and provider is foundational. When viewed as a provider, government steps into the role of supplying goods and services that individuals, acting alone, cannot effectively procure. This perspective sees government as the remedy to collective action dilemmas, where individuals may hesitate to contribute to public goods due to the possibility of others "free-riding" on their contributions. To address this, collective compulsion, often in the form of taxation or regulation, ensures the provision of goods and services that benefit society as a whole.

In this context, critical infrastructure necessary for human connectivity takes center stage. This encompasses not only traditional physical travel infrastructure like roads, bridges, and ports but also modern virtual conduits such as broadband networks. While these infrastructures may initially be developed by private entrepreneurs seeking profit opportunities, their immense capital requirements and widespread societal benefits often prompt government intervention and eventual ownership.

Expanding on this notion, the concept of government as provider extends to the establishment of a social welfare state. Here, the government steps in to support citizens who find themselves unable to fend for themselves, particularly during vulnerable stages such as youth, old age, sickness, disability, and involuntary unemployment. Though critics may view this as a buffer against the harsh realities of capitalism or as a means to safeguard the interests of the wealthy, its fundamental aim is to construct a framework of care that fosters social and economic flourishing, akin to the infrastructure supporting competitive markets. By providing social security, the government empowers citizens to build their own economic stability and pursue opportunities for growth.

Looking towards the future, the trajectory of governance builds upon these core principles of protection and provision. Governments will continue to serve as guardians, shielding citizens from violence and life's adversities, while also fulfilling their role as providers of essential public goods necessary for a globally competitive economy and a cohesive society. However, there's a discernible shift towards investing in citizen capabilities to navigate rapidly evolving circumstances autonomously.

This vision of government as an investor arises from a cultural ethos deeply rooted in entrepreneurship, exemplified prominently in regions like Silicon Valley. Surveys of leading entrepreneurs reveal a desire for government to play an active role in investing in citizens rather than shielding them from the realities of capitalism. They advocate for substantial investments in education, the promotion of active citizenship, the forging of international trade alliances, and the embracing of immigration as means of fostering innovation and economic growth. As highlighted by Alphabet Chairman Eric Schmidt, the convergence of innovation, empowerment, and creativity offers a promising avenue for addressing contemporary challenges.

This celebration of human potential serves as a powerful antidote to prevailing pessimism regarding government's capacity to tackle complex economic, security, demographic, and environmental challenges. Embracing the concept of government as an investor entails more than just allocating funds to education and liberalizing borders; it necessitates a comprehensive investment strategy aimed at nurturing citizen capabilities and providing the necessary resources and infrastructure for citizens to thrive on a grand scale.

INVESTING IN TALENT: NURTURING HUMAN POTENTIAL ACROSS LIFESPANS

Government as an investor carries a profound responsibility, particularly in cultivating the nation's most valuable asset: its human capital. While education undoubtedly stands as a cornerstone, the imperative extends beyond mere schooling to encompass a holistic approach from infancy to old age.

In the formative years, from birth to five, lies a critical juncture wherein the architecture of the brain undergoes rapid development, shaping cognitive abilities and learning potential for a lifetime. Recognizing this pivotal period, the government's investment mandate must encompass a robust infrastructure dedicated to early childhood development. This infrastructure spans prenatal care, ensuring maternal health and nutrition, to postnatal support, including pediatric healthcare services. Moreover, initiatives such as parenting classes and home visitation programs serve to empower caregivers with the knowledge and skills essential for fostering optimal child development. Complementing these efforts are high-quality early education programs tailored to the developmental needs of young children, fostering a solid foundation for future academic success.

Transitioning into adolescence, another phase of profound neurodevelopment, underscores the necessity for tailored interventions and support mechanisms. The teenage years herald not only physical maturation but also cognitive, emotional, and social growth, presenting both opportunities and challenges. In this context, targeted programs offering mentorship, counseling, and extracurricular activities are indispensable for nurturing well-rounded individuals capable of navigating the complexities of contemporary life. Additionally, family support services play a pivotal role in fostering resilience and promoting positive youth development, mitigating the risks associated with adolescent vulnerabilities.

However, the government's role as an investor extends beyond education to encompass the provision of conducive environments for unleashing citizen potential across diverse domains. Drawing from insights by futurists and business strategists, the paradigm of success has shifted from traditional product-centric models to dynamic platforms facilitating collaboration, innovation, and resource access. In this context, government investments must prioritize the creation and maintenance of such platforms, serving as catalysts for individual and collective achievement. Whether in the realms of healthcare, education, entrepreneurship, or beyond, these platforms serve as nexus points where citizens can seamlessly access information, services, and opportunities tailored to their evolving needs and aspirations.

Furthermore, an enlightened approach to investment necessitates a departure from conventional notions of scale and efficiency. While conventional wisdom often equates success with large-scale ventures, the reality is more nuanced. Embracing an anti-scale ethos, government investments should prioritize diversity, resilience, and inclusivity over sheer magnitude. Rather than concentrating resources in a few mega-projects, the emphasis should be on nurturing a vibrant ecosystem of small-scale initiatives, each contributing in its unique way to the social and economic fabric of the nation. From local artisans and family-owned businesses to community-based initiatives and grassroots movements, these diverse endeavors collectively form the bedrock of societal resilience and cohesion.

In essence, a government committed to investing in talent must adopt a multifaceted approach that spans the entire human lifespan. From nurturing early childhood development to supporting adolescent transitions and fostering lifelong learning and innovation, the mandate is clear. By providing the necessary resources, platforms, and support structures, governments can unleash the full potential of their citizens, ushering in an era of prosperity, resilience, and collective well-being.

CHAPTER 2

ECONOMIC PROWESS

Economic growth serves as the barometer of a nation's prosperity, quantified by the expansion of its gross domestic product (GDP). This metric encapsulates the comprehensive value of all goods and services produced within a country's borders over the course of a year. While economic growth is the ultimate goal, its trajectory is influenced by a multitude of intricate factors, rendering it a complex phenomenon to predict or control with absolute precision. Unfortunately, economic downturns, manifested as recessions, are an unavoidable facet of economic cycles, often triggered by external forces such as geopolitical tensions or financial upheavals on a global scale.

In the context of the United States, a nation renowned for its robust economy, the engine of economic growth is driven by the intertwined forces of consumer spending and business investment. Consumer behavior, exemplified by significant purchases like homes, not only fulfills personal needs but also sets in motion a cascade of economic activity. Increased home acquisitions stimulate demand for construction services, thus bolstering the fortunes of home builders, contractors, and construction workers alike. Similarly, businesses play a pivotal role as the architects of economic progress, as they expand operations, hire workers, and make strategic investments to fuel growth.

Consider, for instance, the scenario where a corporation opts to invest in a state-of-the-art manufacturing facility or embraces cutting-edge technologies to enhance productivity. Such initiatives not only create employment opportunities but also catalyze a ripple effect across various sectors of the economy. The infusion of capital into new ventures stimulates job creation and consumer spending, thereby fostering a virtuous cycle of economic expansion.

Beyond the core drivers of consumer spending and business investment, a constellation of ancillary factors synergistically contributes to the overall health of the economy. Financial institutions, such as banks, serve as conduits of economic vitality by extending credit to businesses and individuals. Access to capital empowers enterprises to embark on ambitious ventures, ranging from infrastructure upgrades to product diversification initiatives. Consequently, the ripple effects of such investments reverberate throughout the economic ecosystem, enriching not only the primary stakeholders but also their peripheral counterparts.

In essence, economic growth is a multifaceted phenomenon, orchestrated by a symphony of actors and influences. While consumer spending and business investment serve as the primary drivers, their efficacy is amplified by a supportive infrastructure comprising financial institutions, regulatory frameworks, and technological advancements. By understanding and harnessing the dynamics that underpin economic growth, nations can chart a course towards sustained prosperity and societal well-being.

TAX CUTS AND TAX REBATES

Tax cuts and tax rebates represent strategic maneuvers aimed at bolstering consumers' disposable income. By allowing individuals to retain more of their earnings, these fiscal policies seek to ignite a cycle of economic activity. As consumers find themselves with a surplus of funds, they are inclined to spend a portion of it on goods and services across various sectors. This surge in consumer spending translates into increased revenues for businesses, bolstering their financial health and fostering an environment ripe for growth and expansion.

With a steady influx of revenue, companies are better equipped to invest in vital areas such as capital acquisition and technological advancements. These investments not only enhance operational efficiency but also pave the way for innovation and competitiveness in the marketplace. Moreover, the ripple effects of increased consumer spending and business investments extend beyond individual companies, contributing to broader economic prosperity.

Furthermore, the stimulation of economic activity through tax cuts and rebates is not merely a short-term fix but rather a catalyst for sustained growth. By empowering consumers with greater purchasing power, these measures create a virtuous cycle wherein increased demand drives production, job creation, and further economic prosperity. In essence, tax cuts and rebates serve as potent tools in the economic policymaker's arsenal, harnessing the power of consumer spending to fuel growth, innovation, and prosperity across the economy.

FOSTERING ECONOMIC EXPANSION THROUGH DEREGULATION

Deregulation, the deliberate easing of rules and regulations governing industries or businesses, emerged as a cornerstone of economic policy during the Reagan administration in the 1980s. This shift in approach had a profound impact across various sectors, most notably within the financial realm. Widely regarded as a catalyst for economic dynamism, Reagan's deregulatory initiatives are often credited with fueling the robust growth that characterized the U.S. economy throughout much of the 1980s and 1990s.

Proponents of deregulation assert that overly burdensome regulations act as impediments to business innovation and efficiency. By alleviating regulatory constraints, businesses are afforded greater flexibility to pursue growth opportunities, innovate, and adapt to changing market conditions. Consequently, they argue, this unleashes a virtuous cycle of increased investment, heightened productivity, and expanded employment opportunities, ultimately driving GDP growth.

Conversely, critics of deregulation caution against the risks of excessive laissez-faire policies, pointing to instances where insufficient regulatory oversight has contributed to systemic economic instability. The proliferation of deregulated markets, they argue, can exacerbate market failures and facilitate the emergence of speculative bubbles, leading to volatile boom-and-bust cycles.

The lead-up to the 2008 financial crisis serves as a poignant reminder of the perils of regulatory laxity. The unchecked expansion of the mortgage industry, fueled by the proliferation of subprime mortgages—risky loans extended to borrowers with less-than-ideal credit histories—precipitated a cascading series of defaults and foreclosures, culminating in a full-blown financial meltdown. In response to this crisis, policymakers enacted stringent regulatory reforms aimed at bolstering financial stability, including the imposition of higher capital requirements on banks to fortify their resilience against future shocks.

In essence, the debate over deregulation remains a nuanced and multifaceted one, characterized by competing perspectives on the role of government intervention in shaping economic outcomes. While proponents champion deregulation as a catalyst for innovation and growth, skeptics advocate for prudent regulatory oversight as a safeguard against systemic risks and market excesses. Ultimately, striking the right balance between regulatory flexibility and oversight represents an ongoing challenge for policymakers seeking to foster sustainable economic prosperity.

UTILIZING INFRASTRUCTURE AS A CATALYST FOR ECONOMIC ADVANCEMENT

Infrastructure investment denotes the strategic allocation of financial resources by governmental entities—whether at the local, state, or federal level—to construct or refurbish critical physical assets and amenities essential for fostering the flourishing of commerce and the broader societal ecosystem. These indispensable elements encompass an extensive array of infrastructure, including but not limited to transportation networks such as roads, bridges, ports, and sewage systems, each playing a pivotal role in enabling the seamless functioning of various economic activities and societal functions.

Advocates of infrastructure investment as a potent driver of economic expansion posit that the creation and maintenance of robust infrastructure serve as a linchpin for enhancing overall productivity and competitiveness. By providing a sturdy foundation upon which businesses can operate with maximum efficiency, well-designed and adequately maintained infrastructure not only streamlines logistical operations but also facilitates smoother and more cost-effective movement of goods and services. For instance, the presence of well-constructed roads and bridges not only alleviates traffic congestion but also minimizes transit times for commercial vehicles, thereby reducing operational costs and enhancing supply chain efficiency.

Moreover, investing in infrastructure not only bolsters immediate economic growth but also yields long-term benefits by fostering innovation, attracting investments, and stimulating job creation. Improved infrastructure not only enhances connectivity between regions but also promotes the development of vibrant economic corridors, thereby unlocking new avenues for business expansion and fostering regional economic integration. Furthermore, beyond its economic ramifications, infrastructure investment plays a crucial role in enhancing societal well-being by bolstering public health, safety, and environmental sustainability. Modern sewage systems and sanitation facilities, for instance, not only mitigate health risks but also contribute to environmental conservation by ensuring proper waste management and pollution control.

Basically, leveraging infrastructure as a catalyst for economic growth entails recognizing its multifaceted role as an enabler of productivity, innovation, and societal progress. By prioritizing strategic infrastructure investments, governments can lay the groundwork for sustainable and inclusive economic development, thereby unlocking new opportunities for prosperity and well-being for present and future generations.

ECONOMIC GROWTH ENHANCES STATE CAPACITY AND THE PROVISION OF PUBLIC GOODS IN SEVERAL SIGNIFICANT WAYS.

When economies expand, states can tax the increased revenue, which in turn provides the government with greater financial resources. These resources are crucial for funding and improving essential public services such as healthcare, education, social protection, and basic infrastructure. For instance, with more revenue, a state can build more hospitals and schools, hire additional healthcare workers and teachers, and ensure the maintenance of roads and public utilities. This, in turn, contributes to better health outcomes, higher literacy rates, and overall improved quality of life for its citizens. In addition to the benefits provided by the state, inclusive economic growth leads to broader material gains for the population. As the economy grows, it creates more jobs and business opportunities. This results in higher incomes for both employers and workers. With increased earnings, individuals have more money to spend on goods and services, which stimulates further economic activity. This cycle of increased spending and investment helps people to exit poverty, as they can afford better housing, nutrition, education, and healthcare, thereby significantly improving their living standards.

Furthermore, economic growth can lead to the development of new industries and innovation, which diversifies the economy and makes it more resilient to shocks. This diversification can open up new opportunities for employment and skills development, further enhancing the economic prospects of the population. While economic growth is not the ultimate goal of development, it is a crucial means to achieve it. Effective economic growth strategies should focus on being inclusive, ensuring that the benefits are broadly shared across society rather than concentrated in the hands of a few. This requires policies that promote equitable access to education, healthcare, and economic opportunities, as well as measures to protect the environment and ensure sustainable development. Looking globally, it is evident that countries that have successfully reduced poverty and increased access to public goods have based their progress on strong economic growth. For example, countries like South Korea and Singapore have transformed from low-income nations to high-income economies within a few decades, primarily due to robust economic growth strategies that included significant investments in education, technology, and infrastructure.

In conclusion, while economic growth should not be seen as the ultimate end goal, it is an essential driver of development. By increasing state capacity and providing the necessary resources to supply public goods, economic growth plays a vital role in improving the well-being of citizens and achieving sustainable development.

POLITICS AS A CATALYST FOR ECONOMIC GROWTH

Contrary to what university curricula might suggest, economics and politics are deeply intertwined when it comes to growth. The Effective States and Inclusive Development (ESID) research center's political settlement framework provides an integrated approach to understanding growth and governance. The United States serves as a compelling case study to illustrate this dynamic interplay.

The Role of Political Settlement in the U.S.

The nature of a country's political settlement significantly influences how growth occurs and how the resulting benefits are distributed. This framework prompts critical questions: Do the benefits flow to elite groups or specific societal segments, or are they more widely shared? Do the beneficiaries change with political shifts, or do they remain constant? In the U.S., the political settlement has evolved over time, influencing economic policies and growth patterns. For instance, the New Deal era under President Franklin D. Roosevelt saw a significant shift towards more inclusive economic policies, leading to widespread benefits across various segments of society. Conversely, the neoliberal turn in the late 20th century shifted the benefits towards more elite groups, exacerbating income inequality.

Historical Perspective: The New Deal and Post-War Boom

The New Deal in the 1930s is a prime example of how political settlements can drive economic growth. Faced with the Great Depression, the U.S. government implemented a series of economic reforms and public works projects that reshaped the economic landscape. These policies not only spurred economic growth but also ensured a more equitable distribution of benefits, laying the foundation for the post-World War II economic boom.

Neoliberal Shift: 1980s to Present.

The 1980s marked a significant shift in the U.S. political settlement with the rise of neoliberalism under President Ronald Reagan. This era emphasized deregulation, tax cuts for the wealthy, and reduced government spending on social programs. While this shift led to economic growth, the benefits were unevenly distributed, primarily favoring the wealthy and contributing to rising income inequality.

Modern Implications: The 2008 Financial Crisis and Beyond

The 2008 financial crisis highlighted the critical role of political settlement in economic stability and growth. The crisis, rooted in deregulated financial markets, led to a severe economic downturn. The U.S. government's response, including the Troubled Asset Relief Program (TARP) and subsequent economic stimulus packages, showcased the interplay between politics and economics. These measures stabilized the economy, but debates over their effectiveness and the distribution of benefits persist.

The Role of Political Gridlock

Political gridlock in recent years has further complicated the relationship between politics and economic growth in the U.S. The inability of Congress to pass comprehensive legislation on infrastructure, healthcare, and immigration reform has stymied potential growth. This gridlock reflects deep partisan divisions and highlights the importance of a functional political settlement for sustained economic development.

Inclusive Growth: The Path Forward

To ensure sustained economic growth, the U.S. must address its political settlement to foster more inclusive economic policies. This includes reforms aimed at reducing income inequality, improving access to education and healthcare, and investing in infrastructure. The Biden administration's efforts to pass large-scale infrastructure and social spending bills reflect a recognition of the need for a more inclusive approach to economic growth. The U.S. case study demonstrates that political settlements are crucial in shaping economic growth and the distribution of its benefits. While economic policies are vital, they are deeply influenced by the political context in which they are implemented. Understanding and evolving the political settlement is essential for achieving sustained and inclusive economic growth.

DEALS ARE AS IMPORTANT AS RULES

Understanding Deals versus Formal Institutions

Deals reflect the practical agreements that people rely on, which form the real "rules of the game." Unlike formal institutions—such as laws, regulations, and official policies—deals are the arrangements that individuals and businesses actually adhere to. Formal institutions can often be ignored or corrupted, but deals are the agreements that parties trust and operate by. This distinction is crucial because the ability to rely on deals instills confidence in investors, which is essential for fostering economic progress. Without such confidence, investment—and thus economic growth—tends to be slow and fragmented.

The Role of the State in Economic Development

Effective states are those that can provide ordered deals. Ordered deals are commercial agreements where both parties can trust that the deal will proceed as agreed. This reliability is critical for economic development because it creates a stable environment where businesses can operate and grow. For example, if a business can trust that its contract with the government will be honored, it is more likely to invest and expand, contributing to overall economic growth.

Inclusivity in Deal-Making

A key question in economic development is who gets to make deals. Is it an inclusive process where everyone has a chance, or is it restricted to those with government connections? The inclusivity of deal-making is vital. Different types of economic development require different sorts of deals. While rapid growth can occur without strong institutions, it is imperative that deals are ordered and trusted. Inclusive deals—those that are accessible to a broad group of investors and enterprises—are particularly important. When many investors can participate in economic opportunities, the development process becomes more democratic and sustainable. Deals must evolve from being closed, where only a few connected individuals benefit, to being open, where a wider group of people can engage in economic activities. This shift is essential for achieving structural transformation and sustained inclusive growth.

Collusive Deals and Economic Takeoff

In some scenarios, rapid economic growth can be achieved through collusive deals, where a small group of capitalists collaborates with those in power. This often leads to a quick economic takeoff because of the concentrated investment and streamlined decision-making. However, this approach has significant downsides. When economic growth is driven by close relationships between politicians and capitalists, it often faces challenges later on. Converting initial rapid growth into long-term structural transformation becomes difficult. The economy may struggle to diversify, and the benefits of growth might not be widely shared.

The Path to Sustained Growth

For sustained and inclusive economic growth, it is crucial that deals are both ordered and inclusive. Ordered deals ensure that agreements are reliable, fostering an environment of trust. Inclusive deals ensure that a wide range of participants can engage in economic activities, promoting broader development. Over time, moving from a system of closed, exclusive deals to one of open, inclusive deals is necessary for structural transformation. This transformation leads to more equitable growth, where the benefits of economic progress are widely shared, creating a more stable and prosperous society.

GROWTH CATALYSE STRUCTURAL TRANSFORMATION

1. Inclusive Growth and Structural Transformation:

Inclusive growth refers to economic expansion that benefits all segments of society, particularly the marginalized or disadvantaged groups. It's not just about overall GDP growth but ensuring that the benefits are shared equitably. Structural transformation involves fundamental changes in the economic and social structures of a society. This can include shifts in employment patterns, technological advancements, changes in production processes, and alterations in social norms and institutions.

2. Economic Growth and Social Change:

Economic growth doesn't just lead to more money circulating in the economy; it also triggers broader social changes. These changes can be profound, affecting how people think, work, interact, and organize themselves. For example, technological advancements often accompany economic growth, leading to the creation of new industries and the automation of existing ones. This can alter employment patterns, skill requirements, and social dynamics.

3. Openness and Distribution of Benefits:

Openness in this context refers to an economy's receptiveness to trade, investment, and innovation. A more open economy tends to facilitate the diffusion of new technologies and ideas, fostering structural transformation. Distribution of benefits refers to how the gains from economic growth are shared across different segments of society. Inclusive growth requires that these benefits reach beyond just a privileged few and extend to a broader swath of the population.

4. Role of Capitalists and Technical Abilities:

Capitalists, referring to individuals or entities that invest capital in economic activities, play a pivotal role in driving structural transformation. Their ability to harness new technologies and deploy resources effectively can accelerate economic change. Technical abilities here encompass not only technical skills but also the capacity to innovate, adapt, and take calculated risks in exploring new opportunities.

5. Productivity and Value Creation:

A key aspect of structural transformation is the enhancement of productivity. This involves producing more output with the same or fewer inputs, often achieved through technological advancements, better infrastructure, and improved skills. Shifting towards higher-value goods and services means focusing on industries or activities that generate greater economic value per unit of input. This typically involves moving away from labor-intensive, low-value sectors towards knowledge-based or technologically advanced sectors.

6. Long-Term Poverty Alleviation:

Structural transformation is seen as a pathway to sustainable poverty alleviation. By creating more and better jobs, enhancing productivity, and fostering innovation, societies can lift people out of poverty in a sustained manner. This contrasts with short-term measures that may provide temporary relief but do not address the underlying structural issues that perpetuate poverty.

7. Self-Sufficiency and Reduced Dependence:

As economies undergo structural transformation, companies may become more self-sufficient commercially. This means they rely less on direct support from the state or external sources and are better able to compete in the global marketplace. Reduced dependence on external support can enhance economic resilience and autonomy, contributing to long-term economic stability and growth.

CHAPTER 3

INDUSTRIALIZATION AND PRODUCTION

Industrialization marks the transformative journey of an economy transitioning from predominantly agrarian practices to the mass production of technologically advanced goods and services. It embodies a pivotal phase characterized by profound spikes in productivity, a migration of labor from rural to urban areas, and elevated standards of living. Within this dynamic process, societies experience exponential advancements, both in terms of economic output and social structure. This transition fundamentally reshapes the fabric of societies, heralding a departure from traditional agricultural practices towards mechanized production methods. As industries flourish, they create new opportunities for employment, drawing individuals from rural landscapes into burgeoning urban centers. The resulting urbanization not only alters the geographical landscape but also fosters cultural shifts and new modes of living.

Moreover, industrialization serves as a cornerstone of economic progress, contributing to substantial gains in income per capita and labor productivity. These metrics underscore its significance as a pivotal driver of human development and societal evolution. Indeed, industrialization stands as a defining hallmark of modernity, reshaping economies, societies, and the very trajectory of human history.

The transformative industrial transitions within Western economies unfolded amidst the monumental waves of the 18th and 19th centuries known as the Industrial Revolution. Delving into economic annals, historians frequently highlight four pivotal national industrializations that shaped the trajectory of modernity:

- The seminal industrialization of Great Britain spanning from 1760 to 1840 stands as the cornerstone of the Industrial

Revolution, igniting unprecedented advancements in manufacturing, technology, and societal organization.

- Across the Atlantic, the United States experienced its own profound industrial metamorphosis from 1790 to 1870, characterized by a surge in innovation, mechanization, and infrastructural development, propelling the nation onto the global economic stage.
- Japan, in a remarkable display of industrial prowess, underwent unparalleled advancements from the 1880s to the mid-20th century, marked by a rapid modernization drive that propelled it from feudal isolation to an industrial powerhouse, thereby altering the global economic landscape.

Meanwhile, the monumental industrialization of China, spanning from the mid-20th century to the present era, has reshaped the global economic order, witnessing a staggering ascent from agrarian roots to becoming a manufacturing and technological juggernaut, exerting profound influence on the world stage. These four epochs of industrialization not only reshaped the economic landscapes of their respective nations but also left an indelible imprint on the course of human history, catalyzing unprecedented social, cultural, and geopolitical shifts.

ECONOMIC GROWTH

Economic growth can be generated through several well-established methods. Each method contributes uniquely to increasing the productivity and efficiency of labor and resources within an economy. The primary methods are trade specialization, improved capital goods, and the discovery of previously unutilized resources.

Trade Specialization

Trade specialization involves focusing on specific tasks or activities to enhance proficiency through education, training, and insight. This approach allows workers to become more skilled and efficient in their designated roles. Specialization often occurs naturally as individuals and businesses strive to maximize their gains from trade. For example, a country with a climate conducive to growing coffee may specialize in its production, while another with rich iron ore deposits may focus on steel manufacturing. By concentrating on their respective strengths, both can trade to mutual advantage, thus boosting overall economic output.

Improved Capital Goods

The second method of fostering economic growth is through the enhancement of capital goods. Capital goods refer to the tools, machinery, and equipment used in the production of goods and services. Advancements in these tools can significantly increase productivity per labor hour. For instance, an 18-wheeler truck can transport large quantities of goods over long distances much more efficiently than a bicycle equipped with a backpack. Similarly, modern factory machinery can produce items at a much faster rate and with higher precision than manual labor alone. This increased productivity leads to greater output and economic growth.

Discovery of Previously Unutilized Resources

The third method involves uncovering and utilizing resources that were previously untapped or unknown. Historical examples of this include the discovery of oil wells in the 1850s, which revolutionized energy production and consumption, and the advent of the Internet, which has transformed communication, commerce, and countless other aspects of daily life. The discovery of new resources can provide a substantial boost to the economy by introducing new inputs for production and new avenues for technological advancement and innovation. By leveraging these methods—trade specialization, improved capital goods, and the discovery of new resources— economies can enhance their productivity and achieve sustained economic growth. Each method contributes to creating a more efficient and dynamic economic environment, enabling higher levels of output and improved standards of living.

The cost of acquiring goods declines when more goods can be produced more quickly. This is primarily due to improvements in production efficiency and technological advancements, which allow manufacturers to create more products in less time and at a lower cost. When the real costs of production decrease, these savings can be passed on to consumers in the form of lower prices. As a result, individuals and families find it more affordable to purchase these goods, thereby increasing their overall standard of living. For instance, consider the production of refrigerators. In the early days, refrigerators were expensive and out of reach for most families due to the high costs associated with manual labor and limited production capabilities. However, with the advent of assembly lines and automation, refrigerators can now be manufactured in large quantities at a much lower cost. This reduction in production cost translates to a decrease in the retail price, making refrigerators accessible to a broader range of consumers.

Similarly, the automobile industry has seen significant reductions in costs due to mass production techniques pioneered by companies like Ford. The ability to produce cars quickly and efficiently has made them affordable for the average family, transforming automobiles from luxury items into necessities for modern life. Computers and TVs have followed a similar trajectory. Initially, they were prohibitively expensive and considered luxury items. Advances in technology, such as the development of microprocessors and improvements in manufacturing processes, have drastically reduced the costs associated with producing these electronic goods. Today, computers and TVs are common household items, essential for communication, work, and entertainment. Basic utilities like electricity and running water have also benefited from increased productivity and efficiency in their respective sectors. Investments in infrastructure and technological advancements have made it possible to deliver these services more reliably and at a lower cost, ensuring that more families can enjoy these basic necessities.

In summary, the ability to produce more goods quickly and efficiently leads to lower production costs. These savings are often reflected in the prices consumers pay, making a wide range of goods more affordable. This affordability enhances the standard of living for individuals and families, allowing them to access products and services that were once considered luxuries. Without these increases in productivity, many families would be unable to afford essential items like refrigerators, automobiles, computers, TVs, electricity, and running water.

PROGRESSION OF THE INDUSTRIAL REVOLUTION

The Industrial Revolution marked a period of profound transformation in productivity and economic development, primarily due to significant advancements in capital goods and production techniques. This era witnessed a dramatic rise in marginal productivity, driven by innovations such as the steam engine and the development of more efficient machinery. These technological advancements revolutionized various industries, making it possible to produce a larger quantity of goods at a faster rate.

One of the key innovations of this period was the steam engine, which played a crucial role in mechanizing production and transportation. Steam engines powered factories, mills, and mines, significantly enhancing their output and efficiency. Additionally, the mastery of production techniques, such as the assembly line, streamlined manufacturing processes. The assembly line allowed for the mass production of goods by breaking down production into a series of simple, repetitive tasks performed by workers or machines. This method not only increased the speed of production but also reduced the cost of goods, making them more affordable for the general population. As a result of these technological and procedural advancements, the output of goods increased exponentially. The ability to produce more goods in less time meant that economies could support larger populations with better quality and variety of food, which in turn fueled population growth and helped combat malnutrition. The improvements in agricultural and industrial productivity ensured that more people had access to sufficient and nutritious food, laying the foundation for a healthier and more robust workforce. Furthermore, the increased efficiency in production freed up time for other pursuits. With the basic necessities more readily available, people had more time to dedicate to education, innovation, and leisure activities. This shift not only improved the quality of life but also fostered a culture of continuous improvement and creativity, leading to further advancements and economic growth.

The rise in average real incomes during the Industrial Revolution was another significant outcome. As productivity soared, so did the wages and living standards of many workers. This increase in disposable income spurred greater demand for a variety of goods and services, creating a positive feedback loop of economic expansion. People began to seek out and afford higher quality products, driving industries to innovate and improve their offerings continuously. The Industrial Revolution was characterized by a remarkable increase in productivity due to technological innovations like the steam engine and efficient production techniques like the assembly line. This led to higher output, better food supply, population growth, and improved living standards. The era laid the groundwork for modern industrial economies and significantly enhanced the quality of life by allowing more time for education, innovation, and leisure, while also driving a continuous cycle of economic growth and development.

MODES OF INDUSTRIALIZATION

Industrialization has been achieved through various strategies and methods over time, each yielding different levels of success. The approaches can be broadly categorized into several distinct phases and strategies.

Early Industrialization: Mercantilism and Protectionism

The Industrial Revolution in Europe and the United States began under mercantilist and protectionist policies. Governments played a significant role in fostering industrial growth by implementing protective tariffs and regulations to shield emerging industries from foreign competition. These policies created a nurturing environment for nascent industries, allowing them to develop and mature. As these industries grew stronger, there was a gradual shift towards a laissez-faire or free-market approach. This shift encouraged foreign trade by reducing trade barriers, thereby opening up new markets for industrial goods and facilitating the exchange of technology and ideas.

Post-Second World War: Import-Substituting Industrialization

In the aftermath of the Second World War, many developing nations in Latin America and Africa adopted a strategy known as import-substituting industrialization (ISI). This strategy aimed to reduce dependency on imported goods by fostering domestic production. Governments implemented protectionist measures such as high tariffs and import quotas to protect local industries from foreign competition. Additionally, there were direct interventions in the economy through subsidies and, in some cases, the nationalization of key industries. The goal was to build self-sufficient economies that could produce a wide range of goods domestically. However, this approach often led to inefficiencies and a lack of competitiveness, as protected industries had little incentive to innovate or improve productivity.

Export-Led Growth: East Asia and Parts of Europe

Around the same time, several East Asian economies, along with parts of Europe, pursued a different strategy known as export-led growth. This strategy focused on developing industries with the potential to compete in global markets. Governments played a supportive role by investing in infrastructure, education, and technology to enhance industrial capacity. A key element of this strategy was maintaining a weak currency, which made exports cheaper and more competitive on the international market. By deliberately pursuing foreign trade, these countries built robust export-oriented industries. The emphasis on quality and competitiveness drove continuous improvement and innovation, leading to sustained economic growth.

Comparative Outcomes

In general, the export-led growth strategy has proven more successful than import-substituting industrialization. Countries that embraced export-led growth, such as South Korea and Taiwan, experienced rapid industrialization and significant improvements in living standards. Their industries became globally competitive, leading to long-term economic stability and prosperity. In contrast, countries that relied on import substitution often struggled with economic inefficiencies and slower growth rates. Their protected industries failed to achieve the competitiveness needed to thrive in the global market, resulting in economic stagnation and dependency on imported technologies and capital goods. Overall, while both strategies aimed to achieve industrial growth, the export-led approach has consistently outperformed import-substituting industrialization in terms of economic outcomes and sustainability.

SOCIALIST INDUSTRIALIZATION IN THE 20TH CENTURY

In the 20th century, socialist nations undertook ambitious centrally planned programs aimed at rapid industrialization. Notable examples include the Soviet Union's first and second Five-Year Plans and China's Great Leap Forward. These programs aimed to shift their economies towards a more industrial base and significantly increase the output of industrial commodities. However, these efforts were not without severe consequences. The implementation of these plans often involved strict government control and repression. Workers faced deteriorating living and working conditions, and in some cases, such as during the Great Leap Forward, these policies led to widespread famine and starvation.

Key Examples of Industrialization

Industrialization depends heavily on growth and innovation across multiple industries. Here are some key industries and their contributions:

Manufacturing

The dawn of industrialization began with groundbreaking inventions that significantly boosted manufacturing capabilities.

- **The Cotton Gin**: Patented by Eli Whitney in 1794, the cotton gin revolutionized the process of separating cotton seeds from cotton fibers. Whether hand-cranked or steam-powered, it dramatically increased the speed and efficiency of cotton processing.

- **The Spinning Jenny:** This invention allowed a single spinner to operate multiple spindles simultaneously, greatly enhancing the production of cotton and woolen threads.
- **The Steam Engine**: Perhaps the most pivotal invention, the improved steam engine by James Watt in 1763, harnessed coal power to drive machinery, playing a crucial role in the Industrial Revolution.

Mining

The mining industry saw several key innovations in the 19th century that supported the broader industrialization process.

- **Steam Engine for Pumping Water:** The first practical use of the steam engine was to pump water out of coal and tin mines, allowing deeper extraction of resources without flooding.

- **Steam Locomotives:** Initially developed to transport ore from mines, these locomotives facilitated the movement of large quantities of raw materials.
- **Dynamite**: Patented in 1867, dynamite was used to clear rock obstructions in mining operations, enabling more efficient extraction of minerals.

Transportation

The 19th century witnessed significant advancements in transportation, which were crucial for industrialization.

- **Steam Locomotives:** Stephenson's Rocket, introduced in 1829, became the model for future locomotives. These engines were essential for transporting raw materials and finished goods across long distances.
- **Steamboats**: The adaptation of steam technology to boats revolutionized the transport of goods and people along rivers, greatly enhancing trade and mobility.

Retailing

The retail sector also saw innovations designed to cater to the growing consumer market of the 19th century.

- **Department Stores**: John Wanamaker's store, opened in Philadelphia in 1887, was one of the first department stores, offering a wide range of goods under one roof and transforming the shopping experience.
- **Sears Catalog**: While not the first mail-order catalog, the Sears catalog was notable for its extensive reach, offering a vast array of products to consumers across America, including children's clothing and prefabricated houses. These innovations across various industries collectively fueled the

process of industrialization, transforming economies and societies in profound ways.

Job Creation and Urban Migration

Industrialization significantly impacts society by creating a multitude of jobs, which draw people from rural areas, such as farms and villages, to urban centers where manufacturing and industrial activities take place. For many, these industrial jobs, despite being physically demanding and sometimes hazardous, offer a more stable income compared to the uncertain and often harsh life of subsistence farming. The promise of regular wages and better living conditions drives large-scale migration to cities.

Emergence of Urban Consumers

As people move to urban areas, they transform into a new generation of urban consumers. This demographic shift spurs the growth of various businesses that cater to the needs of city dwellers. From food vendors and clothing stores to entertainment venues and service providers, a diverse array of enterprises emerges to meet the demands of the burgeoning urban population. Consequently, the economy diversifies and expands, creating a vibrant marketplace.

Growth of the Middle Class

Industrialization fosters the development of a larger middle class. This group comprises artisans, shopkeepers, and professionals who benefit from the increased economic activity in urban areas. With more disposable income and better living standards, the middle class becomes a significant force in society, contributing to cultural, social, and economic changes. Their demand for goods and services further stimulates economic growth and innovation.

Challenges for the Working Class

However, industrialization also leads to the formation of a substantial working class, which often faces grueling working conditions. Factory jobs typically involve long hours, low wages, and unsafe environments. The lack of worker rights and protections during the early stages of industrialization results in significant hardships for many laborers. The disparity between the wealthy industrialists and the impoverished workers becomes starkly evident.

Labor Unions and Worker Rights

The harsh conditions experienced by the working class during the Industrial Revolution give rise to the labor union movement. Workers begin to organize and advocate for better wages, reasonable working hours, and safer working conditions. Labor unions become a powerful force for change, leading to significant reforms and the establishment of labor rights. This movement lays the foundation for modern labor laws and protections that continue to shape the workforce today.

CHAPTER 4

AGRICULTURE

The term "agriculture" finds its roots in the Latin word "ager" or "agri," referring to soil, combined with "culture," signifying the cultivation of the land. In its contemporary understanding, agriculture encompasses the intricate blend of both art and science, dedicated to nurturing the soil, cultivating crops, and raising livestock.

Delving deeper, farming can be viewed as a comprehensive system with distinct phases encompassing inputs, processing, and outputs. Beginning with inputs such as seeds, fertilizers, and machinery, the process progresses through a series of operations including ploughing, sowing, irrigation, weeding, and ultimately, harvesting. These operations constitute the pivotal stages in transforming raw agricultural resources into final outputs, which encompass a diverse array of products ranging from crops to dairy and poultry items.

HOW AGRICULTURE COULD TRANSFORM A NATION AND ITS PEOPLE

Agriculture stands as the cornerstone of Belize's economy, contributing significantly to both national and local levels with its diverse array of fruits, vegetables, and root crops. However, in the Stan Creek district, a gap exists in the flow of information and communication between local markets and farmers. This void results in highly inefficient production cycles, where farmers rely on intuition rather than market demands, leading to substantial waste. Overproduction or underproduction often leads to erratic price fluctuations, causing economic instability and food insecurity. This deficiency serves as the impetus for our thesis project in Dangriga, where our aim is to synchronize market demands with agricultural production. By doing so, we seek to streamline production, reduce food costs, minimize waste, and alleviate food insecurity. Moreover, our endeavor aims to foster connections between local farmers, market vendors, and consumers, fostering market stability and reducing chaos.

GLOBAL CONTEXT

The agricultural sector plays a pivotal role in propelling a nation towards high-income status and economic transformation. This sector not only ensures food security and nutrition but also serves as a catalyst for overall development. History underscores the significance of prioritizing agriculture to accelerate economic growth while addressing hunger and malnutrition. For instance, China's remarkable economic ascent was underpinned by agricultural transformation, showcasing the pivotal role of agriculture in uplifting nations. Agriculture not only fosters economic prosperity but also addresses pressing issues like malnutrition and food insecurity, making it a linchpin for social progress.

The agricultural workforce arguably constitutes the most crucial production force in developing countries, with a significant portion of the rural population depending on it for livelihood. However, many rural farmers grapple with limited education, poor health, and poverty, hindering their potential and impeding community well-being. Insufficient and inaccurate information exacerbates economic uncertainty, leading to price fluctuations, reduced income for farmers, and heightened food insecurity. Moreover, price volatility exacerbates child labor, further straining families already grappling with financial hardship. Additionally, the absence of accurate information hampers crop planning, adversely affecting community health and exacerbating food insecurity.

The significance of information as a tool for empowerment cannot be overstated. Access to information is crucial for survival and can be transformative, particularly in agriculture. Information empowers individuals, dispels ignorance, and fosters enlightenment, thereby driving progress. However, limited access to information, be it educational resources, community data, or public policies, detrimentally impacts communities, hindering their development potential. Information serves as the lifeblood of modern society, playing a pivotal role in facilitating progress across various domains. In agriculture, access to accurate information is paramount for enhancing productivity and fostering sustainable growth, ultimately bolstering rural livelihoods, ensuring food security, and bolstering national economies.

BELIZE CONTEXT

Despite boasting conducive agricultural conditions, Belize contends with higher rates of undernourishment, growth stunting, and obesity compared to its Central American counterparts. This phenomenon, known as the 'double burden of malnourishment' and 'Obesity Paradox,' underscores the complex interplay between food insecurity and health outcomes. A significant portion of the Belizean population grapples with poverty, with a considerable proportion of youth classified as multi-dimensionally poor. Moreover, a substantial segment of Belizean children lacks access to basic necessities such as adequate nutrition, clean water, sanitation, housing, and education. Given agriculture's pivotal role in the Belizean economy, stakeholders recognize its potential to uplift both the nation and its people. The World Bank underscores agriculture's significance in income generation, employment, food security, and poverty alleviation in Belize. Agriculture also intersects with tourism, as establishments like hotels, resorts, and restaurants serve as major buyers for locally produced goods. Furthermore, agriculture constitutes a significant portion of both formal and informal occupations, particularly in rural areas.

In 2015, the Belizean government, in collaboration with various entities, identified five pillars to enhance the agricultural sector. These pillars encompass sustainable production, market development, food security, sustainable agriculture, and governance. Our project focuses on the third pillar, emphasizing national food security and rural livelihoods, with the overarching goal of bolstering local production and reducing dependence on food imports.

DEMAND SURVEY AND ANALYSIS

To address the aforementioned challenges and support the local community, our team initiated two buyer demand surveys targeting local market vendors. These surveys, comprising a mix of qualitative and quantitative questions, aimed to glean insights into market preferences and demand dynamics. By engaging vendors in conversations and meticulously documenting their responses, we fostered a collaborative atmosphere conducive to information exchange. Surprisingly, we encountered Spanish-speaking immigrants operating a significant portion of the surveyed markets in Dangriga, highlighting the importance of linguistic diversity in research endeavors. After consolidating quantitative data and visualizing demand patterns, we delved into the qualitative insights gathered during interviews. Vendors consistently highlighted key issues such as delivery reliability, product consistency, and variety. To address these concerns, we formulated recommendations aimed at fostering closer collaboration between farmers and vendors. Central to our recommendations was the establishment of direct communication channels between these stakeholders, enabling vendors to procure goods directly from farmers. Such relationships not only ensure a steady supply for vendors but also provide farmers with a reliable market outlet and invaluable demand insights.

As relationships between farmers and vendors deepen, opportunities emerge for cost savings and quality improvements throughout the supply chain. By reducing intermediary costs and enhancing supply chain efficiency, local farmers can offer high-quality products at competitive prices, benefiting both vendors and consumers. Moreover, facilitating direct connections between producers and buyers aligns with the goal of enhancing national food security by promoting local production and reducing reliance on imports.

Government Involvement and Vendor Perspectives

Reflecting on government interventions in agricultural markets, our surveys revealed vendor concerns regarding import bans, which, while aimed at supporting local farmers, inadvertently disrupt supply chains and compromise product quality. Vendors emphasized the need for policy measures that prioritize competitiveness and information dissemination over protectionist measures. Additionally, vendors expressed hope for continued engagement from the Ministry of Agriculture through ongoing surveys and dialogue, underscoring the importance of sustained collaboration between stakeholders.

REFLECTIONS

Concluding our project, I gained profound insights into the intricacies of agricultural dynamics and community engagement. This experience transcended mere academic pursuit, instilling valuable lessons in empathy, cultural immersion, and grassroots collaboration. Unlike the prevailing ethos in the United States, where professional identity often defines individuals, Belizean culture emphasizes human connection and holistic well-being. This realization prompted a paradigm shift in my personal and professional aspirations, emphasizing the importance of meaningful engagement and societal impact over material pursuits. Moreover, the project underscored the transformative potential of hands-on work, particularly in developing contexts. Immersed in the local community, we recognized the paramount importance of building trust and fostering genuine connections to drive sustainable change. This grassroots approach not only enriched our understanding of local realities but also laid the foundation for enduring partnerships and collective progress.

In closing, I extend my gratitude to the University of Arkansas, PeaceWorks, and Dr. Amy Farmer for facilitating this transformative experience. Special thanks to the Belize Ministry of Agriculture and all stakeholders for their invaluable collaboration, which exemplifies the power of collective action in advancing agricultural development and community well-being. As we conclude our project, I remain committed to the ongoing pursuit of inclusive, impactful initiatives that uplift communities and foster sustainable development.

PROVIDING RAW MATERIALS

Raw materials are the essential substances that form the foundation of the global economy. They are indispensable for manufacturing and production processes across various industries. Without these materials, it would be impossible to produce the wide array of products we rely on daily. Nonagricultural raw materials include critical elements such as steel, which is used in construction and manufacturing; minerals, which are essential for electronics and other high-tech industries; and coal, which is a significant energy source.

Agricultural raw materials also play a crucial role. For instance, lumber from trees is used extensively in construction. Herbs and spices, derived from plants, add flavor to food and have medicinal uses. Corn is a versatile crop, serving as both a food product and a base for ethanol, a type of biofuel that provides an alternative to fossil fuels. Resins, which are plant-derived substances, are utilized in many industrial applications such as adhesives and coatings, particularly in the construction industry. These examples illustrate the diverse applications and importance of raw materials in sustaining economic activities and development.

CREATING A STRONG SUPPLY CHAIN

The global supply chain is a complex network that ensures the movement of goods, including agricultural products, from producers to consumers. Efficient logistics and transportation methods, such as ocean freight, rail, and trucking, are vital to this process. Any disruptions or delays in the supply chain can have significant consequences. For example, if agricultural products are delayed at a port in Los Angeles, it can create a bottleneck that affects markets across the globe, including in China. Conversely, delays in other parts of the world can impact the availability of goods in the United States. A concrete instance of this is the 2021 surge in soybean sales from Iowa. This increase was partly due to delays in the shipment of South American crops, which gave Iowa a competitive edge. However, while such situations can benefit one region, they can also be detrimental to others, causing shortages and affecting economic stability.

ENCOURAGING ECONOMIC DEVELOPMENT

Agriculture is not just about producing food; it is a vital component of the global economy with far-reaching impacts. It supports job creation and stimulates economic growth across various sectors. According to USAID, countries with robust agricultural sectors often see growth in employment beyond just farming, as related industries such as processing, transportation, and retail also expand.

Moreover, nations that focus on increasing agricultural productivity and developing strong agricultural infrastructure tend to experience higher per capita incomes. This is because agricultural innovation, through advanced technologies and improved farm management practices, leads to increased efficiency and profitability. This, in turn, promotes broader economic development and raises the standard of living for the population. The agricultural sector's ability to drive innovation and productivity highlights its critical role in fostering sustainable economic growth and development globally.

FIVE RELEVANCES OF AGRICULTURE TO THE NATION

Agriculture is a cornerstone of global economies and societies, impacting a wide range of sectors and providing essential products that sustain daily life, industry, and sustainability. Here's a detailed exploration of its multifaceted contributions:

1. Food Production

Fruits and Vegetables

Fruits and vegetables are indispensable for human nutrition. They are primary sources of essential vitamins such as A, C, and E, and minerals like magnesium, zinc, and phosphorus. These nutrients are critical for maintaining health, preventing diseases, and promoting overall well-being. Moreover, fruits and vegetables are rich in dietary fibers, proteins, and carbohydrates, making them fundamental components of a balanced diet. They also enhance culinary diversity by adding unique flavors and textures to meals, enriching the human diet.

Animal Feed

Agricultural products are not only consumed directly by humans but also used extensively as animal feed. This includes grains, hay, straw, sprouted grains, and legumes, which are essential for the growth and health of livestock. The American Industry Feed Association reports that about 900 animal feed ingredients are legally approved in the U.S. These feeds support the production of meat, dairy, and poultry products, ensuring a steady supply of protein-rich food sources for human consumption. Efficient and sustainable animal feed production is crucial for maintaining the balance in the food supply chain and supporting the agricultural economy.

2. Industrial Raw Materials

Natural Rubber

Natural rubber is a critical raw material, especially in the automotive industry. It is primarily used in the manufacture of tires, which are essential for over 1.4 billion vehicles globally. The major rubber-producing countries—Thailand, Indonesia, and Malaysia—collectively account for approximately 70% of global natural rubber production. This industry is predominantly supported by small-scale farmers, highlighting its socio-economic importance. Natural rubber's elasticity, durability, and resistance make it indispensable for various industrial applications beyond tires, including footwear, medical supplies, and consumer goods.

Cotton

Cotton is a fundamental agricultural commodity in the textile industry. The journey from cotton fields to clothing involves multiple stages: growing, harvesting, processing, spinning, and weaving. Cotton represents about 31% of all textile fibers globally, underscoring its significance in the production of a wide range of apparel and household items. The cultivation and processing of cotton support millions of jobs worldwide, from farmers to factory workers, and drive substantial economic activity in both developing and developed countries.

3. Energy Production

Biofuels

Biofuels, derived from biomass such as corn, soybeans, sugarcane, and algae, offer a renewable alternative to fossil fuels. The U.S. Environmental Protection Agency (EPA) highlights the economic and environmental benefits of biofuels, which include reduced greenhouse gas emissions and pollutants. Biofuels can help diversify energy sources, enhance energy security, and support rural economies by providing additional income streams for farmers. However, the production of biofuels requires significant land and water resources, potentially impacting food availability and prices. Balancing biofuel production with food security remains a critical challenge.

4. Industrial and Chemical Products

Bio-based Chemistry

Bio-based chemistry involves the transformation of agricultural raw materials into industrial products. These bio-based products include bioplastics, plant oils, biolubricants, inks, dyes, detergents, and fertilizers. Unlike conventional products derived from petroleum, bio-based products are more sustainable and environmentally friendly. They contribute to reducing the carbon footprint of industrial activities and promote the principles of green chemistry by minimizing the use of hazardous substances and waste. The development and use of bio-based chemicals are crucial for advancing sustainable industrial practices and reducing reliance on non-renewable resources.

5. Healthcare and Pharmaceuticals

Medicinal Plants

For thousands of years, humans have relied on plants for medicinal purposes. Today, many pharmaceutical products are still derived from plant sources. For example, the foxglove plant produces digoxin, a drug used to treat heart failure. Another significant example is polylactic acid (PLA), produced from the fermentation of glucose in green plants. PLA has diverse medical applications, including tissue engineering, cardiovascular implants, orthopedic interventions, cancer therapy, and the fabrication of surgical implants. The use of plant-derived substances in pharmaceuticals underscores the importance of agriculture in healthcare, providing natural alternatives and complements to synthetic drugs.

Agriculture's vast contributions extend beyond food production, playing a critical role in sustaining industrial, energy, and healthcare sectors. Its integration into global supply chains highlights the need for sustainable agricultural practices and innovations to meet the evolving demands of a growing population.

CHAPTER 5

MILITARY STRENGHT AND WEAPON

One of the few core responsibilities of the federal government, as mandated by the Constitution of the United States, is "to provide for the common defence." Upon commissioning, every American military officer swears an oath to "support and defend" this Constitution. This underscores the fundamental mission of the American military: to protect and defend the nation. This mission involves deterring potential aggressors and, if deterrence fails, fighting and winning wars. Any discussion regarding the military's role and American defense policy must begin with this foundational principle. However, the need for a strong military extends beyond the mission to fight and win wars. As Theodore Roosevelt's quote at the beginning of this essay illustrates, American leaders have long recognized that a formidable military can yield significant diplomatic and economic benefits, even—especially—when not engaged in wartime activities. Over the past century, the United States' military capability has supported the nation's rise to global prominence. This rise was often due to the increased influence and credibility derived from military strength rather than the direct use of force. Throughout this period, an American strategic tradition developed, integrating military strength with diplomatic skill, economic growth, and international influence. This tradition has a distinguished heritage and continues to be relevant today.

Historical records show that a strong national defense bolsters national power and global influence in many ways beyond the kinetic use of force. A robust defense budget and policy enhance our nation's capabilities and influence across virtually all other elements of national power: our economy, our diplomacy, our alliances, and our credibility and influence in the world. Conversely, an underfunded national defense threatens to diminish our national power across all of these dimensions. A strong national defense is therefore indispensable for a peaceful, successful, and free America—even if a shot is never fired. The diplomatic successes the United States has achieved in building and maintaining a stable and peaceful international order over the past century have been enabled by America's military dominance. Conversely, the significant defense budget cuts and the corresponding rise of potential peer competitors in recent times are already undermining America's diplomatic and economic influence.

A well-equipped military improves diplomacy with adversaries, strengthens our alliances, signals credibility and resolve, deters aggression, and enhances national morale. However, the benefits of a strong military extend beyond these direct effects. There are multiple pathways by which investments in military hard power produce economic benefits. For instance, the military's role in protecting a stable international environment creates predictable and secure conditions conducive to economic growth. The American security umbrella facilitated Western Europe's postwar reconstruction and economic revival. Similarly, Asia's half-century economic boom has been partly a result of America's treaty alliances in the region, which maintain peace and stability. This stability is exemplified by the United States Navy's Seventh Fleet, which protects an open maritime order, ensures freedom of navigation, and secures sea lanes. Moreover, while America's world-leading economy has largely been driven by free enterprise and private sector–led growth, innovations in defense technology have often had economically beneficial civilian applications. Numerous technological innovations from the past 75 years originated as defense projects before being adapted for private-sector commercial use. These include nuclear energy, jet propulsion, the Internet, global positioning systems, and unmanned aerial vehicles.

PEACE THROUGH STRENGTH

One of President Ronald Reagan's favored mantras, often cited even today, was "peace through strength." Embedded in this slogan is a complex set of strategic assumptions. For example, it suggests that a strong military can be effective without being deployed in hostile action, that the acquisition of arms can inversely correlate with their use, that military strength pays diplomatic dividends, and that preparedness for war enables the preservation of peace. United States Military Academy professor Gail Yoshitani describes Reagan's formulation of the "peace through strength" strategy: Peace was not simply the absence of war. Instead, it was conceived as a world hospitable to American society and its liberal-democratic ideals in which the United States and its allies were free from the threat of nuclear war and had access to vital resources, such as oil, and vital transportation and communications routes. Reagan believed that such a peace was dependent upon US strength, which would come from rebuilding the nation's economic and military might.

This strategic concept is rooted in the tradition of Theodore Roosevelt from eight decades earlier. For Roosevelt, as for Reagan and many other American leaders, "peace" meant more than just the absence of conflict. It encompassed the full flourishing of American interests and ideals, predicated on an expansive concept of national "strength" that included diplomatic, ideological, economic, and military dimensions.

The Three Ds: Defense, Diplomacy, and Development

In recent years, the Obama Administration introduced a new strategic concept, not in direct contradiction to "peace through strength" but aimed at recalibrating American national security policy. This concept, known as the "three Ds" of defense, diplomacy, and development, seeks to diminish the focus on national defense and elevate the importance of international development. As then-Secretary of State Hillary Clinton stated in her January 22, 2009, inaugural remarks:

Development must become an equal pillar of our foreign policy, alongside defense and diplomacy. The three Ds must be mutually reinforcing. While this concept appropriately recognizes the relationship between sustainable development and improved peace and security, it skews the triad by making development co-equal with defense. Ironically, despite the Obama Administration's intention to elevate development policy, the implementation has had the opposite effect, marginalizing development and diminishing defense policy, evidenced by significant cuts in the defense budget over the past six years.

Primacy of National Defense

Both constitutionally and conceptually, a strong national defense should take primacy over development. A well-equipped military creates an enabling environment for improved development policy. Many notable economic development successes over the past 75 years occurred within the context of either an explicit American security umbrella or a more favorable security environment underwritten by American defense policy. Examples include the economic successes of postwar Western Europe, post-Cold War Central and Eastern Europe, the "Asian Tigers" (Japan, South Korea, Taiwan, and Singapore), and the unprecedented growth and poverty alleviation in China since Deng Xiaoping's 1979 economic reforms and India since Manmohan Singh's 1991 economic liberalization. All took place in the context of American troop presence, explicit American security guarantees, or a stable regional environment supported by American power projection. This observation is not meant to disparage economic development or the work of development professionals, which should be a national priority on moral, humanitarian, and strategic grounds. Rather, it highlights that economic development efforts are most successful and enduring when undertaken in a context of peace and stability, typically provided by a guarantor of security backed by military power.

Military Power and National Security

The broader sweep of American history and international politics reinforces the perception that military power enables diplomatic and economic progress. This historical insight is especially relevant today. Each of the major national security policy challenges facing the United States—including growing Chinese assertiveness in the western Pacific, a revanchist Russia destabilizing the postwar European order, the collapse of the state system in the Middle East, resurgent jihadist groups like the Islamic State and various al-Qaeda franchises, Iran's nuclear ambitions and regional hegemonic aspirations, and North Korea's expanding nuclear capabilities—has its own complex internal and external causes. However, all these challenges have been occurring in the context of global perceptions of a diminished and weakened American defense capability, which in turn undermines American diplomatic and economic power and influence. The setbacks for American foreign policy in recent years vividly illustrate both the non-kinetic utility of military power and the costs when it is diminished.

STRENGTHENING DIPLOMACY AND NATIONAL MORALE (THEODORE ROOSEVELT)

Introduction: America's Emerging Global Power

If the 19th century was marked by the United States expanding and solidifying its continental control, resolving internal conflicts through the Civil War, the early 20th century signaled America's turn outward as an emerging global power. Theodore Roosevelt, occupying the

White House during these pivotal years, played a crucial role in this transformation.

Roosevelt's Foreign Policy Vision

Roosevelt's foreign policy was characterized by a combination of assertive military buildup and deft diplomacy, balancing credible displays of force with restraint in its actual use. He significantly increased the defense budget, focusing primarily on building up the Navy, reflecting his belief in the primacy of naval power for strategic force projection. One scholar of Roosevelt's foreign policy encapsulated his approach: "Power and diplomacy work best when they work together."

The Great White Fleet: A Bold Display of Naval Power

One of the most vivid illustrations of Roosevelt's foreign policy was his decision to send 16 American battleships on a 14-month voyage around the world in 1908. This display of naval strength, known as the "Great White Fleet," was unprecedented since Chinese Admiral Zheng He's 15th-century voyages. As historian H. W. Brands noted, "Nothing like this had ever been attempted. For the United States to be the first to accomplish it would be a cause for national pride.... Never before had so much naval power been gathered in one place, let alone sent on a grand tour around the globe."

Bolstering National Morale

Roosevelt intuitively understood that an expanded global role for the United States required popular support. Demonstrating the Navy's capabilities was a means to inspire national pride and unity. As Roosevelt himself stated, "my prime purpose was to impress the American people; and this purpose was fully achieved." He drew on the insights of his friend, naval strategist Alfred Thayer Mahan, who believed that "national character" was a critical element of sea power.

Impact on National Morale and Civic Unity

The Great White Fleet's circumnavigation served multiple purposes: showcasing America's industrial might, technological prowess, audacity, and intrepid spirit. It was also a strategic move to garner public support for the United States' emerging international leadership role. Roosevelt's demonstration of naval power was not merely for show but aimed to foster national morale and civic unity, reminding Americans of their country's strengths.

Aimed at International Audiences

Roosevelt's display of naval power was intended for international as well as domestic audiences, particularly targeting Japan and Germany. He recognized Japan's growing power and ambitions, which led him to mediate the Treaty of Portsmouth, ending the Russo-Japanese War and earning him the Nobel Peace Prize. Despite his admiration for Japan, Roosevelt was wary of its regional ambitions and potential threats to American territories. Years earlier, he had even directed the Naval War College to plan for a scenario involving Japanese aggression towards the Hawaiian Islands.

Strategic Communication to Japan

Roosevelt's Great White Fleet was a strategic signal to Japan, reminding them of America's Pacific power. Despite critics' concerns that such displays might provoke conflict, Roosevelt believed that strength was less provocative than weakness. As he stated, "The only thing that will prevent war is the Japanese feeling that we shall not be beaten, and this feeling we can only excite by keeping and making our navy efficient in the highest degree."

Message to Germany

While Germany's aggression would later lead to World War I, Roosevelt was already wary of Kaiser Wilhelm's ambitions. During a diplomatic dispute, Roosevelt highlighted the fleet's progress to the German leader, implicitly emphasizing American naval capabilities. His message underscored the strategic importance of military power in diplomatic relations.

Roosevelt's Doctrine: Military Power and Diplomatic Acumen

Roosevelt's presidency is notable for its peaceful expansion of American influence, achieved through a sophisticated understanding of the interplay between military strength and diplomacy. He believed that a robust military deterred aggression and maintained peace. In his 1905 address to Congress, Roosevelt argued against disarmament, stressing that a strong military was essential for ensuring a just peace.

Conclusion: Enduring Legacy

Roosevelt's insights remain relevant today. He famously advocated for "speak softly and carry a big stick," translating this aphorism into a strategic doctrine. A strong military can enhance national power and influence, often without the need for actual force. This capability depends on perceptions of American credibility, combining both military power and the willingness to use it if necessary. Roosevelt's legacy emphasizes the importance of maintaining a formidable military to support diplomatic efforts and ensure national security.

Signaling Resolve and Supporting Allies (Harry S. Truman)

At first glance, Presidents Theodore Roosevelt and Harry Truman appear to have little in common. Roosevelt, a Republican, hailed from the East Coast and was a Harvard-educated blue blood from a distinguished family lineage. Truman, a Democrat, came from a small town in the Midwest and was a haberdasher with only a high school education, making him the last American president without a college degree. Roosevelt was the architect of America's debut at the high table of international politics, while Truman found himself as the somewhat bewildered inheritor of America's new role as a global superpower, having to build many of the institutions that defined the postwar international order.

However, Roosevelt and Truman shared significant commonalities, including a belief in American exceptionalism, a commitment to the universality of liberty, and a determination to preserve and extend free societies. Both presidents recognized the importance of a strong military in projecting power and influence, often without resorting to lethal force. Truman, like Roosevelt, achieved enduring national security accomplishments through the strategic use of military power as a diplomatic and economic instrument of statecraft. The international institutions and postwar order Truman helped create still benefit the nation today, offering valuable lessons in integrating a strong defense into a broader structure of national power.

Upon assuming the presidency in April 1945, Truman faced an unprecedentedly complex situation. He quickly had to navigate several monumental challenges:

- **The Decision to Drop the Atomic Bomb on Japan:** This decision ended World War II but also initiated the nuclear age, posing profound ethical and strategic dilemmas.
- **Post-War Reconstruction:** Truman oversaw the unconditional surrender settlements of Germany and Japan, giving the U.S. near-total control over their reconstruction.
- **Crafting a Postwar Order:** He aimed to create an international political and economic system that would preserve stability and promote prosperity and ordered liberty.
- **The Cold War:** The emerging Cold War with the Soviet Union required strategies to contain Soviet expansionism and prevent a nuclear war.

Navigating these challenges would have tested the most seasoned statesman, let alone Truman, a relatively untested and seemingly ill-equipped Senator from Missouri.

To appreciate Truman's strategic innovations, it's crucial to understand the tense and unprecedented international climate of his time. Although the United States and the Soviet Union were allies during World War II, tensions over the postwar order emerged as the war wound down in 1945. By 1946, it was evident that Soviet leader

Josef Stalin viewed the United States as an adversary with designs on dominating Eastern Europe and beyond. American leaders faced the dilemma of either confronting the Soviet Union or acquiescing to the spread of Communist tyranny. Historian John Lewis Gaddis described this period as "the despair of 1946 when war or appeasement appeared to be the only alternatives open to the United States." Furthermore, there were fears that the end of the war might lead to a return of the economic depression of the 1930s. Amidst this anxiety and policy uncertainty, diplomat George Kennan sent his renowned "Long Telegram" from Moscow, diagnosing Soviet intentions and advocating a strategy of containment. This strategy proposed resisting Soviet aggression without triggering another world war. While Kennan conceptualized containment, it was Truman's leadership that operationalized and implemented it.

The success of containment relied heavily on the non-kinetic use of military power. Kennan himself noted the importance of military presence in diplomacy, famously stating in a 1946 address at the National War College, "You have no idea how much it contributes to the politeness and pleasantness of diplomacy when you have a little quiet armed force in the background." He later emphasized that military strength was essential for making political positions credible, deterring attacks, encouraging allies, and waging war successfully if necessary. Truman's Cold War policy integrated these insights. His administration created a national and international framework that leveraged military power into diplomatic and economic influence, as seen in initiatives like the Marshall Plan, the creation of NATO, the National Security Act (which established the CIA and National Security Council), and strategy blueprints such as NSC-68. Two initiatives especially highlight this concept: the Truman Doctrine and the Berlin Airlift.

In his 1947 address to Congress, Truman declared that "it must be the policy of the United States to support free peoples who are resisting attempted subjugation by armed minorities or by outside pressures." This declaration led to aid packages for Greece and Turkey that included substantial military components, helping these nations defeat Communist insurgencies. Truman's advisers debated limiting the aid to economic support, but Truman, influenced by Under Secretary of State Dean Acheson, insisted on including military hardware and advisers. This approach, termed "armed diplomacy" by political scientist Henry Nau, had far-reaching implications, such as the establishment of the Joint American Military Mission to Aid Turkey (JAMMAT), transforming the Turkish military and setting a precedent for future U.S. military assistance programs. The robust military aid to Greece and Turkey demonstrated Truman's use of military resources to support allies and signal American resolve to the Soviet Union. This aid was possible due to the military expertise and technology developed during World War II, despite rapid postwar demobilization. Truman's integration of military hardware, economic aid, and diplomacy into a cohesive strategy marked a new era in American power projection.

In 1948, Truman faced another significant challenge when the Soviet Union blocked Western access to West Berlin. Rather than capitulating diplomatically or escalating militarily, Truman ordered a massive airlift to supply the beleaguered city. For 11 months, American cargo planes delivered food, medicine, and essentials, until Stalin lifted the blockade. This non-kinetic military operation signaled American resolve and reassured West Berliners, showing that the U.S. was committed to defending freedom in Europe. Henry Nau noted that Truman's decision to sustain Berlin was monumental, placing American forces at risk to defend the borders of freedom in Europe. This strategic use of military resources without direct confrontation revealed Soviet intentions and limitations, galvanized American allies, and led to the formation of NATO. Through these actions, Truman effectively used military power to achieve diplomatic successes and demonstrate American strength, setting the stage for future Cold War strategies and reinforcing the United States' role as a global superpower.

THE IMPORTANCE OF MILITARY POWER IN THE 21ST CENTURY

International Strategic Analysis (ISA) continues its in-depth examination of the global balance of power, meticulously assessing the relative strength of countries and political entities worldwide. Last year, ISA unveiled its Country Power Rankings, an ongoing project that will see an updated release later this year. In the interim, ISA is set to publish new reports and forecasts concerning the global balance of power in the coming months. Among the various forms of power that define a country's global standing, military power is perhaps the most immediately apparent to the general public. A nation with a robust military typically enjoys heightened security and stability compared to a state with weaker military capabilities, especially relative to its neighbors and potential adversaries. Moreover, military supremacy allows a nation to assert or diminish another state's power in other domains, such as economic, political, or resource-based power. Historically, military power has often been the driving force behind a nation's ascent to great power status. Conversely, the lack of military strength has led to the downfall of states that either were once great powers or had the potential to become so but failed. History is replete with examples of states whose ultimate demise was sealed on the battlefield, even if the decline began in other areas of power.

DETERMINANTS OF MILITARY POWER

Several factors contribute to a nation's overall military strength:

1. Offensive Military Power: This involves a nation's capability to project force beyond its borders aggressively, significantly influencing its overall power.

2. Defensive Military Power: This measures a nation's ability to defend its territory against aggression from rival countries, coalitions, or non-state actors.

3. Land Power: Historically the dominant form of military strength, land power remains crucial despite the rising importance of naval, aerial, and space warfare.

4. Sea Power: Most of history's greatest powers have commanded significant advantages in naval warfare, crucial for global influence.

5. Air Power: Although just over a century old, air power is now vital to a nation's military capabilities and is expected to continue growing in importance.

6. Advanced Military Power: This encompasses technologies such as weapons of mass destruction, cyber-warfare, and space capabilities, whose disruptive potential will likely increase their significance.

7. Allies: The great wars of recent centuries have demonstrated that strong, reliable allies significantly bolster a nation's military power and its prospects in conflicts.

FACTORS SUPPORTING MILITARY POWER

In addition to direct military capabilities, several other factors are vital in sustaining military power:

1. Economic Strength: A nation must have the economic resources to afford the high costs and technological advancements necessary for maintaining military power.

2. Demographic Health: A large, healthy population provides the necessary manpower for sustaining a military force, though automation may eventually change this dynamic.

3. Environmental and Natural Resources: Geographic advantages and resource wealth are crucial for defense and military projection.

4. Political Stability: Political strength and unity are reflected in the stability and effectiveness of the armed forces.

5. Technological Innovation: Technological advancements have historically determined the outcomes of conflicts, favoring the more advanced states.

6. Cultural Factors: A cultural emphasis on military values can enhance a nation's military power, while cultural resistance can impede it.

Interplay Between Military Power and Other Power Factors

Military power also significantly influences other areas of a nation's overall power:

1. Economic Impact: Secure territories and trade routes provide economic advantages, while military power can also drive economic growth.

2. Demographic Protection: A strong military can safeguard the population, promoting healthy demographic growth.

3. Resource Control: Military power allows nations to protect or acquire environmental and resource wealth.

4. Political Influence: Armed forces have historically played a crucial role in political stability, enhancing political power when relations are stable.

5. Technological Development: Military needs often spur technological innovations, which can have broader societal benefits.

6. Cultural Influence: While military power has a limited direct impact on cultural power, dominant military states often impose their cultural norms on others.

HISTORICAL EXAMPLES AND MODERN IMPLICATIONS

Throughout history, many nations have leveraged military power to achieve great power status. For instance:

Macedonia: Under Philip II and Alexander, military advancements propelled Macedonia from obscurity to dominance among Greek states.

Russia: Despite being considered a minor state, Prussia's military strength enabled it to unify Germany and become Europe's leading power.

Soviet Union: Its military foundations helped it rise as a global superpower post-World War II.

However, excessive focus on military power has also led to the downfall of some great powers:

Roman Empire: Over-investment in the military drained resources, contributing to its decline.

16th-17th Century Spain: Similarly, Spain's heavy military expenditure undermined its other strengths.

Soviet Union: The unsustainable military burden played a role in its collapse.

On the other hand, insufficient military investment has also led to significant losses:

- Byzantine Empire: Military weakness allowed Arab forces to capture much of its territory.
- China: Military decline enabled the Mongol conquest in the 13th century.
- France: Inadequate military power relative to Germany resulted in the loss of its leadership in Europe.

Contemporary Military Power

Today, there is a stark disparity in military power among the world's leading nations. The United States remains dominant, spending more on its military than the next eight largest spenders combined. However, the U.S. has learned that its military might is not sufficient to maintain dominance in multiple global regions simultaneously. China is emerging as a formidable military rival. Although its military power still lags behind the U.S., Chinese defense spending now exceeds one-third of U.S. expenditure, with the gap expected to narrow. Other countries lag significantly behind the U.S. and China in projecting continuous military power far from their borders. Thus, the United States and China continue to be the dominant military powers of the 21st century, a trend likely to persist in the foreseeable future.

CHAPTER 6

POPULATION

A growing population can place significant stress on the environment, transportation systems, and the provision of essential natural resources such as water, food, and energy, particularly when governments fail to think strategically or are slow to implement necessary adaptive reforms. Ineffective management of these resources can lead to their scarcity and environmental degradation, both of which pose serious challenges to sustainable development initiatives. However, if appropriate policies are adopted, a growing population can also drive economic expansion and result in a larger labor force, which is beneficial for sustainable development. It is crucial to ensure that economic progress is balanced with environmental conservation and the safeguarding of natural resources. This requires the integration of sustainable practices into policy-making to support both the economy and the environment simultaneously.

Effective strategic planning and timely reforms can transform population growth into an asset rather than a liability. Governments must prioritize sustainable resource management, invest in renewable energy, and promote efficient transportation systems to mitigate the negative impacts of population growth. Additionally, policies that encourage responsible consumption, protect natural habitats, and enhance resource efficiency are essential for maintaining a balance between economic development and environmental stewardship.

Global Population Milestone and Future Projections

On November 15, 2022, the global population surpassed 8 billion people, marking a historic milestone in human demographics. However, this is just a waypoint on a continuing upward trajectory. Demographers and experts in population studies project that the global population will increase to 8.5 billion by 2030, representing a growth of 500 million people in just eight years. This rapid increase is set to continue, with expectations that the world population will reach 9.7 billion by 2050. By the end of the 21st century, projections suggest that the global population will exceed 10 billion.

Concentration of Population Growth in Developing Regions

A significant portion of this population growth is anticipated to occur in low- and lower-middle-income countries. These regions are characterized by higher fertility rates compared to high-income countries, which often have aging populations and lower birth rates.

Demographic Dynamics in Africa

Africa, in particular, is a focal point for this projected population boom. The continent has experienced one of the highest growth rates globally due to several factors:

- High Birth Rates: African countries consistently report some of the highest birth rates in the world. Cultural, social, and economic factors contribute to larger family sizes.
- Declining Mortality Rates: Improvements in healthcare, nutrition, and sanitation have significantly reduced mortality rates. Diseases that once claimed many lives, particularly among children, are now better managed or eradicated in many regions.

- Youthful Population: Africa has a very young population, with a high proportion of people in the childbearing age group, contributing to sustained high birth rates.

As a result of these factors, Africa's population has grown almost tenfold over the past century. Currently, the continent is home to over 1.4 billion people. According to United Nations projections, this number is expected to swell to approximately 2.5 billion by 2050. This rapid population increase presents both challenges and opportunities.

Implications of Rapid Population Growth

The anticipated population growth in developing regions, particularly in Africa, carries significant implications for various aspects of society and development:

- Economic Development: Rapid population growth can spur economic growth through an expanded labor force. However, it also requires substantial investment in education, healthcare, and infrastructure to ensure sustainable development.
- Urbanization: As populations grow, urban areas are likely to expand, leading to the growth of megacities. This urbanization process needs to be managed to avoid issues such as overcrowding, pollution, and inadequate housing.
- Resource Management: More people mean increased demand for resources such as food, water, and energy. Sustainable management of these resources is crucial to prevent shortages and environmental degradation.
- Healthcare and Education: With more children being born, there is a pressing need to expand and improve healthcare and educational services. Ensuring that the growing population is healthy and well-educated is vital for future economic and social stability.

- Environmental Impact: Increased population pressure can lead to environmental challenges, including deforestation, loss of biodiversity, and increased greenhouse gas emissions. Implementing sustainable practices and policies is essential to mitigate these impacts.

THE POSITIVE AND NEGATIVE EFFECTS OF POPULATION GROWTH ON SUSTAINABLE DEVELOPMENT

Global population growth has a complex impact on sustainable development, encompassing both positive and negative effects. While an increasing population can drive economic growth by boosting demand for goods and services, it can also lead to higher costs and significant challenges to sustainability.

Negative Effects

- **Resource Shortages**: As the population grows, the demand for essential resources such as food, energy, and water increases. This heightened demand can lead to shortages and competition for these limited resources, potentially resulting in higher prices and conflicts over resource allocation.
- **Environmental Issues:** Population growth contributes to environmental degradation in multiple ways. More people means more pollution from industrial and domestic sources. Increased deforestation to create living space and agricultural land destroys habitats and reduces biodiversity. Additionally, overfishing and mining activities escalate, further harming ecosystems.
- **Urbanization:** Rapid population growth often leads to the expansion of urban areas, resulting in overcrowded cities. This urban sprawl can lead to the development of slums, increased waste production, and significant stress on existing infrastructure such as transportation systems, sewage, and water supply networks.

- **Healthcare:** A larger population demands more healthcare services, which can be challenging to provide. Inadequate healthcare infrastructure and insufficient medical personnel can lead to lower quality care and increased disease prevalence, especially in developing regions.
- **Climate Change:** Increased population results in higher consumption levels, particularly in high-income countries where lifestyle and consumption patterns are resource-intensive. This escalates greenhouse gas emissions, contributing to global warming and climate change. The environmental footprint of a growing population exacerbates the already critical issue of climate change.

Positive Effects

- **Larger Workforce:** A growing population increases the labor force, which is vital for economic expansion. More workers can mean higher productivity and the potential for increased economic output, fostering sustainable development if managed properly.
- **Innovation and Economic Growth:** An expanding population creates a larger market for goods and services, which can drive innovation. Companies are motivated to develop new products and improve existing ones to meet the diverse needs of a growing consumer base, leading to economic growth and technological advancements.
- **Diversity:** Population growth often brings together people from various racial, ethnic, and cultural backgrounds. This diversity can lead to a richer exchange of ideas and perspectives, fostering creativity and innovation. A diverse population can also promote social cohesion and mutual understanding, enhancing social stability and inclusive development.
- **Talent Pool:** A larger population increases the number of educated and skilled individuals. This expanded talent pool

can support sustainable development by providing the necessary human capital for businesses and industries to innovate, grow, and compete globally.

- **Global Cooperation:** As the population grows, the need for international cooperation and coordination becomes more critical. Addressing global challenges such as resource management, environmental protection, and economic development requires collaborative efforts. Population growth can thus drive countries to work together more closely, fostering global partnerships aimed at sustainable development.

In summary, while population growth presents significant challenges to sustainable development, it also offers opportunities for economic growth, innovation, and global cooperation. Balancing these effects requires careful planning and international collaboration to ensure that development remains sustainable and inclusive.

THE IMPACT OF HIGH-INCOME COUNTRIES ON SUSTAINABLE DEVELOPMENT.

The United Nations report on the impact of population growth on sustainable development reveals some surprising insights. Contrary to popular belief, high-income nations generally have lower rates of population growth. However, these nations have extremely high levels of resource consumption per person. This includes the use of energy, water, and raw materials. Such high levels of resource use can strain the planet's limited resources and hinder other countries' efforts to achieve sustainable development.

Resource Consumption and Global Strain

High-income countries consume a disproportionate share of the world's resources. For example, residents of these nations use more energy for heating, cooling, transportation, and manufacturing. They consume more water for domestic, agricultural, and industrial purposes. They also use large amounts of raw materials for building infrastructure, producing goods, and maintaining their high standards of living. This excessive consumption depletes natural resources, many of which are finite, and can lead to environmental degradation, including deforestation, water scarcity, and loss of biodiversity.

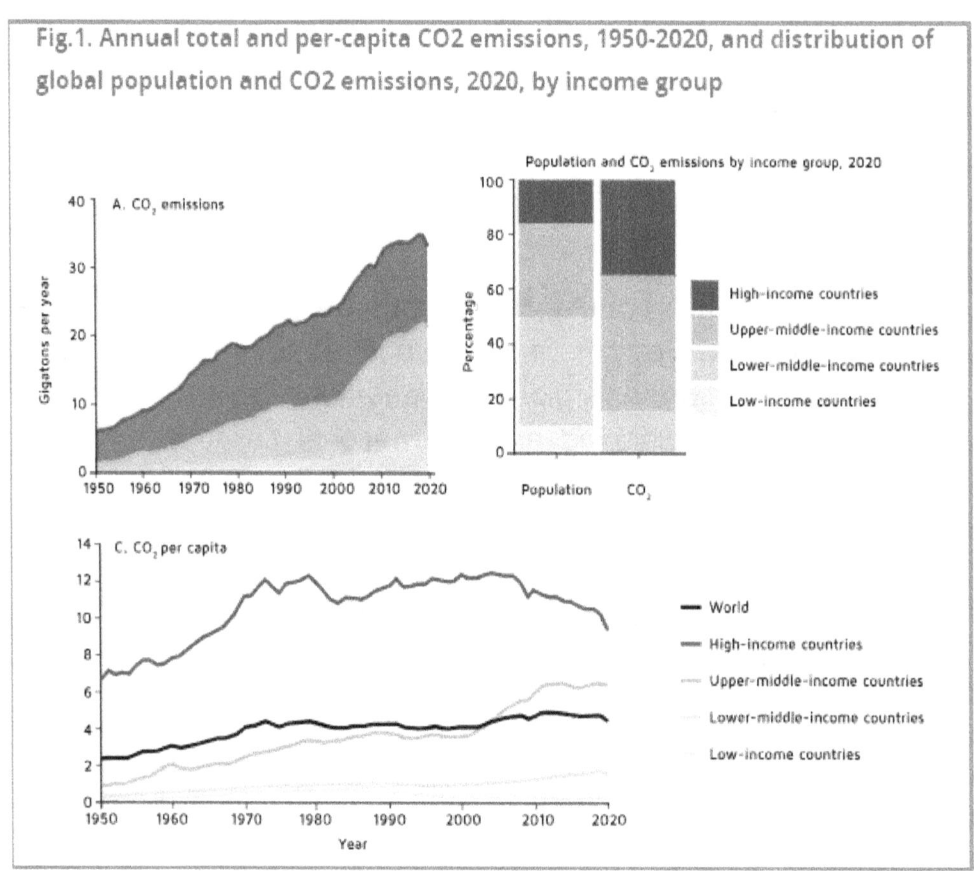

Emissions and Climate Change

Population growth, combined with the industrial revolution and modern consumption patterns, significantly contributes to greenhouse gas emissions. The industrial revolution marked the beginning of large-scale use of fossil fuels, which continues to this day, leading to high emissions of carbon dioxide (CO2) and methane (CH4). These gases are major contributors to global warming and climate change. Modern consumption patterns, characterized by high demand for energy-intensive products and services, further exacerbate this issue.

It is important to note that the highest per capita greenhouse gas emissions come from high-income countries. These nations have advanced industrial sectors, widespread use of personal vehicles, and high levels of energy consumption in households and businesses. As a result, they emit far more greenhouse gases per person compared to low-income countries, where average incomes are lower and populations are growing more rapidly.

Global Warming and Vulnerable Nations

High-income nations, being significant contributors to global warming, create challenges for low-income countries that are striving for sustainable development. Many low-income nations are already at risk because they have limited ability to adapt to and mitigate the effects of climate change. These countries often lack the financial resources, technology, and infrastructure necessary to respond effectively to climate-related impacts such as extreme weather events, sea-level rise, and changing agricultural conditions. For example, small island nations and countries with large coastal populations are particularly vulnerable to sea-level rise, which can lead to loss of land, displacement of people, and damage to infrastructure. Similarly, countries in arid and semi-arid regions may experience increased droughts, which can affect water supplies, agriculture, and food security. Without adequate support and resources, these nations face significant hurdles in their efforts to achieve sustainable development.

THE IMPACT OF POPULATION GROWTH ON RESOURCE DEMAND AND AGRICULTURE

The continuous growth of the global population significantly increases the demand for various resources, particularly food. This surge in food demand exerts pressure on essential resources such as land, water, and energy. To meet this heightened demand, there is a greater reliance on chemical fertilizers and pesticides, which in turn can lead to soil degradation over time. In areas where subsistence farming is prevalent—where farmers grow crops mainly for their own consumption and that of their families—the need for additional agricultural land becomes pressing. Due to the lack of adequate irrigation, high-quality seeds, and soil enhancement techniques, farmers are compelled to clear more land for cultivation. This expansion often leads to deforestation, which adversely affects biodiversity, soil health, and the global carbon balance.

Agricultural Impacts on Biodiversity and Ecosystems

The expansion of agricultural activities necessitated by population growth frequently results in habitat loss, further endangering biodiversity. However, adopting sustainable agricultural practices can mitigate these negative impacts. By reducing the use of harmful chemicals and employing methods that support ecosystems, sustainable agriculture can help preserve biodiversity and maintain ecological balance.

Changes in Consumption Patterns and Environmental Impact

As populations grow and average incomes rise, dietary habits shift, leading to an increase in the consumption of calorie-dense and resource-intensive foods such as beef, dairy products, poultry, pork, and eggs. These dietary changes have a substantial environmental impact, contributing to higher greenhouse gas emissions, further biodiversity loss, and increased water and soil pollution due to inadequate environmental management practices.

Strategies for Addressing Food Insecurity

To effectively tackle hunger and food insecurity, governments need to develop comprehensive strategies that emphasize sustainable agricultural practices. These strategies should focus on enhancing agricultural productivity without resorting to intensive, environmentally harmful methods. Key components of such a strategy include:

- Reducing food loss and waste
- Improving infrastructure and supply chains within the food system
- Promoting agricultural techniques that are environmentally sustainable
- By prioritizing these areas, governments can work towards ensuring food security while preserving environmental health and promoting sustainable development.

10 POSITIVE EFFECTS OF POPULATION GROWTH ON ECONOMIC DEVELOPMENT

- **Expanded Labor Force**

Population growth leads to an expanded labor force, increasing the number of individuals available and willing to work. This larger labor pool provides businesses with access to a wider range of skills, talents, and abilities. As more people enter the workforce, productivity and efficiency across various sectors improve. Businesses can expand their operations, take on larger projects, and increase their output to meet the growing consumer demand, contributing significantly to economic growth.

- **Increased Tax Revenue**

A larger population generally leads to increased economic activity and consumption, resulting in higher tax revenues for governments. This additional revenue can be invested in critical areas such as infrastructure, education, healthcare, and public services. For example, improved transportation systems like roads, bridges, airports, and public transit can create jobs, stimulate short-term economic activity, and enhance long-term economic productivity by facilitating the efficient movement of goods and people.

- **Market Expansion**

Population growth expands the potential consumer base, creating a larger market for goods and services. Businesses benefit from increased demand, which can drive them to expand their operations, increase production capacity, and innovate new products. This market expansion not only boosts sales and revenue but also encourages competitiveness and technological advancements, further driving economic growth.

- **Technological Advancements**

A growing population can foster innovation and technological development. With more individuals entering the workforce, there is a greater pool of potential inventors, scientists, and researchers. Increased human capital promotes the generation of new ideas and breakthrough discoveries, leading to advancements in various fields such as information technology, healthcare, renewable energy, and transportation. Collaborative efforts among diverse individuals further accelerate knowledge-sharing and technological progress.

- **Enhanced Human Capital**

Population growth enhances human capital by increasing the number of individuals available for education and skill development. A larger population demands more educational and training programs, resulting in expanded educational institutions and vocational training centers. This improved access to education equips individuals with the knowledge and skills necessary for productive employment. A well-educated and skilled workforce enhances productivity and drives economic growth across various sectors.

- **Economic Diversification**

Population growth stimulates economic diversification by creating increased demand for various goods, services, and employment opportunities. This demand encourages the development of new industries and the expansion of existing ones, reducing dependence on a single sector. For instance, growth in population may lead to higher demand for housing, healthcare, education, and entertainment, fostering the growth of construction, healthcare, education, hospitality, and retail sectors, thereby enhancing economic resilience and sustainability.

- **Urbanization and Infrastructure Development**

As the population grows, so does the demand for housing, services, and employment opportunities, driving urbanization and infrastructure development. Urban areas become hubs of economic activity, attracting businesses and investments. This concentration of economic activities fosters innovation and productivity, leading to higher wages and improved living standards. The development of infrastructure such as transportation networks, utilities, and public facilities supports the growing urban population, enhancing connectivity and economic efficiency.

- **Cultural and Knowledge Exchange**

A larger population brings together individuals from diverse cultural, social, and educational backgrounds, fostering an environment rich in cultural and knowledge exchange. This diversity promotes creativity and innovation as people share unique perspectives and ideas. Cultural exchange enhances creativity in arts, technology, and science, while knowledge exchange leads to the development of innovative solutions to complex problems, driving economic and societal progress.

- **Entrepreneurship and Small Business Growth**

Population growth increases the demand for goods and services, creating opportunities for entrepreneurs to address market needs. A larger consumer base motivates entrepreneurs to identify market gaps and develop innovative solutions. The growth of small businesses contributes to job creation, innovation, and economic vitality. New businesses provide unique products and services, catering to diverse customer preferences and driving economic growth.

- **Long-Term Investment and Economic Stability**

Population growth encourages long-term investment in infrastructure, education, healthcare, and other essential sectors. As the population expands, the need for adequate infrastructure becomes critical to support housing, transportation, and utilities. Governments and private investors recognize this need and invest in developing transportation networks, utilities, and public facilities. Such investments improve connectivity, enhance productivity, attract businesses, and stimulate economic activity, leading to sustainable economic growth and stability.

CHAPTER 7

TECHNOLOGY

Advancements in technology possess the transformative potential to cultivate a fairer, more peaceful, and just world. With digital progress at our disposal, we can effectively bolster the pursuit of each of the 17 Sustainable Development Goals. These objectives span from the eradication of extreme poverty to the mitigation of maternal and infant mortality rates, the promotion of sustainable agricultural practices and equitable employment opportunities, and the realization of universal literacy. Yet, alongside their promise, technologies also harbor the capacity to encroach upon privacy, compromise security, and exacerbate societal disparities. They wield significant influence over human rights and agency, presenting a complex web of ethical considerations and challenges.

In this pivotal moment, akin to generations that came before us, we – encompassing governments, businesses, and individuals alike – are faced with a critical choice. It is incumbent upon us to deliberate deliberately on how we choose to harness and navigate the realm of emerging technologies. Through proactive and conscientious management, we can steer the trajectory of technological innovation toward a future that is equitable, secure, and conducive to the advancement of humanity.

IMPACT OF DIGITAL TECHNOLOGY

Digital technologies have surged forward at an unprecedented pace, outstripping any other innovation in human history. Within just two decades, they've reached approximately half of the developing world's population, fundamentally reshaping societies in their wake. By bolstering connectivity, fostering financial inclusion, expanding access to trade and public services, technology has emerged as a potent equalizer.

Consider the healthcare sector: AI-powered technologies at the forefront are revolutionizing disease diagnosis, saving lives, and extending life expectancies. In education, virtual learning platforms and distance education have broken down barriers, offering educational opportunities to students previously marginalized. Public services are undergoing a transformation, becoming more accessible and transparent through blockchain-powered systems and less encumbered by bureaucracy with the assistance of AI. Additionally, big data is revolutionizing policymaking, enabling more agile and precise policy formulation and program implementation. However, while the benefits of this digital revolution are profound, there remains a significant segment of the population disconnected from its advantages, perpetuating existing inequalities. Women, the elderly, persons with disabilities, ethnic or linguistic minorities, indigenous groups, and residents of impoverished or remote areas often find themselves left behind. Moreover, the pace of connectivity is decelerating, and in some cases, regressing, particularly among certain demographics. Globally, women's internet usage lags behind men's by 12%, with the gap widening in the least developed countries. The use of algorithms, while offering great potential, also poses risks. Algorithms can replicate and exacerbate human and systemic biases when operating on inadequately diverse datasets.

Furthermore, the lack of diversity in the technology sector hampers efforts to address these challenges effectively.

THE FUTURE OF WORK

Historically, technological revolutions have reshaped the labor force, creating new job opportunities, rendering others obsolete, and catalyzing broader societal transformations. The current wave of technological change is poised to have profound ramifications. For instance, the shift toward a greener economy could generate 24 million new jobs globally by 2030 through the adoption of sustainable practices. However, reports indicate that automation could result in 800 million job losses by 2030, sparking concerns among employees about lacking the necessary skills for well-paid employment. Addressing these trends necessitates a reevaluation of education, emphasizing STEM subjects, soft skills, and resilience. Lifelong learning and upskilling are imperative, given the evolving nature of work. Additionally, unpaid work, such as childcare and elderly care, requires better support, especially given the aging global population.

THE FUTURE OF DATA

Digital technologies, such as AI and data pooling, are utilized for various purposes, from tracking agricultural and environmental issues to mundane tasks like paying bills. However, they also have the potential to infringe upon human rights, through surveillance and data exploitation. Establishing better regulation of personal data ownership could transform personal data into an asset, empowering individuals and safeguarding their rights.

THE FUTURE OF SOCIAL MEDIA

Social media, connecting nearly half of the global population, serves as a platform for voices to be heard worldwide in real-time. However, it also harbors risks, amplifying hate speech, misinformation, and reinforcing echo chambers. While social media algorithms have the potential to either unite or fragment societies, their impact remains profound.

THE FUTURE OF CYBERSPACE

The management of these technological developments is a topic of intense debate amid escalating geopolitical tensions. The prospect of a 'great fracture' between world powers, each with its own internet and AI strategies, threatens to erect a digital Berlin Wall. As such, fostering digital cooperation between nations and establishing universal cyberspace standards is crucial for a united world. A 'global commitment for digital cooperation' emerges as a key recommendation in addressing these challenges.

HOW TECHNOLOGY IS HELPING ECONOMIES IN DEVELOPING COUNTRIES

The rapid spread of globalization has been significantly accelerated by the Internet and other advancements in communication technology. For developing countries, access to these technologies offers numerous benefits, with one of the most significant being the potential to boost a nation's economy. Technology helps economies in developing countries by reducing production costs, fostering the growth of new businesses, and enhancing communication.

However, developing countries face challenges that need to be addressed to fully benefit from technology. One major issue is the need to prioritize technological innovation rather than merely adopting existing technologies. Additionally, there must be an equitable distribution of technology across the entire country, as currently, poorer populations often lack the same level of access. To address these issues, it is crucial for organizations to monitor technological advancements and promote innovation and job creation. One organization that strives to address these challenges is Broadband for Good. This group provides internet access to rural areas and supports programs that leverage technology to drive community development. By bringing the internet to underserved regions, Broadband for Good helps bridge the digital divide and promotes inclusive progress.

When used effectively, technology can significantly enhance economic prosperity. An illustrative example of this is found in India, where the Self-Employed Women's Association (SEWA) uses SMS technology to send agricultural workers updates on commodity prices. This timely information enables farmers to make informed decisions about where to sell their produce, leading to increased income as they can access broader markets. Another notable initiative in India is the Hand in Hand Partnership (HIHP). This organization empowers women by providing them with mobile devices and training to launch their own tech-driven businesses. By offering technical support and encouraging women to develop innovative ideas, HIHP fosters sustainable economic growth and long-term empowerment.

Similar success stories can be found in countries like Nigeria, Egypt, and Indonesia. In these nations, micro-entrepreneurs contribute significantly to the economy, with 38 percent of their gross domestic product (GDP) being generated by small businesses. A 2011 World Bank report highlighted that small businesses are crucial for job creation and innovation, both of which are vital for economic development.Overall, while developing countries face challenges in accessing and utilizing technology, targeted efforts by organizations and initiatives can lead to substantial economic benefits and a more equitable distribution of technological advancements.

THE PIVOTAL AND EVER-INCREASING ROLE OF TECHNOLOGY IN NATION BUILDING

Introduction

Daniel Bell, a renowned professor emeritus of sociology, eloquently described technology in his collection "The Winding Passage: Essays and Sociological Journeys, 1960-1980," as "a soaring exercise of the human imagination." He emphasized that technology, much like art, bridges culture and social structure, reshaping both in the process. A review of technological evolution since the dawn of human civilization and its transformative impact on human lives and behaviors substantiates his words.

Historical Perspective on Technological Evolution

Human civilizations have greatly benefited from technological innovations and inventions across the ages. Thriving and evolving civilizations have invariably witnessed significant technological innovation, influenced by the aspirations and ideals of their populations. This symbiotic relationship between society and technology creates a cycle where technological advancements drive societal changes, which in turn foster further technological innovations. Technological advancements have profoundly changed societal behaviors and operations, impacting social, political, and economic environments and fueling further technological demands. The proverb "necessity is the mother of invention" aptly describes this dynamic, with societal needs being the primary driver behind technological inventions. Technology enhances efficiency, alters human adaptive mechanisms, and accelerates human evolution.

Definition and Scope of Technology

The Encyclopaedia Britannica defines technology as "the application of scientific knowledge to the practical aims of human life or, as it is sometimes phrased, to the change and manipulation of the human environment." Technological innovations span from ancient inventions like the wheel and agriculture to medieval tools like the compass and chariots, to modern-day computers, mobile phones, and robots. Future technologies promise even more advancements, including advanced smart devices, quantum computers, blockchain technologies, smart cities, and sophisticated applications of artificial intelligence. Technology permeates every component of civilization, affecting language, education, architecture, city planning, communication, military, health, and record-keeping.

Celebrating Technological Achievements in India

In India, the Ministry of Science and Technology celebrates National Technology Day on May 11th each year. This day symbolizes the quest for scientific inquiry, technological creativity, and the integration of science, society, and industry. It commemorates the achievements of scientists and engineers, particularly highlighting India's successful nuclear tests at Pokhran. The tests, codenamed 'Operation Smiling Buddha' (1974) and 'Operation Shakti' (1998), marked India's emergence as a nuclear power. The day also celebrates other significant technological milestones, such as the test flight of the indigenous aircraft 'Hansa-3' and the test firing of the 'Trishul' missile system. Each year, the day is celebrated with a specific theme; for 2023, it is "School to Startups - Igniting Young Minds to Innovate."

IMPACT OF MODERN TECHNOLOGY

- **Education:** Technology has revolutionized education, making learning accessible and convenient. Computers and the Internet provide information and resources around the clock. Online education platforms offer unprecedented opportunities for earning degrees and learning new skills from anywhere in the world. Initiatives like PM eVIDYA, DIKSHA, SWAYAM Prabha, and others have further expanded digital education in India, ensuring quality education for all students.
- **Communication:** Technological innovations have transformed communication, making it instant and accessible. From ancient methods like smoke signals and letters to modern instant messaging and video conferencing, technology has made communication more effective and convenient. Apps like Zoom, Skype, and Google Teams played crucial roles during the pandemic by enabling remote work and education.

- **Health:** Advances in medical technology have increased life expectancy and quality of life. Modern diagnostic tools, vaccines, and treatments for chronic conditions have revolutionized healthcare. Initiatives like the Ayushman Bharat Digital Mission aim to create a digital health ecosystem, providing digital health IDs and integrated health records.
- **Transportation:** Innovations in transportation, from trains and cars to airplanes, have made travel more feasible and comfortable. Ridesharing apps like Uber and Ola have further simplified travel. In India, organizations like CSIR and CRRI contribute to advancements in transportation technology, including electric vehicles and biofuels.
- **Banking:** Technology has transformed banking, making transactions easier and faster. Online banking and payment apps like Google Pay and PayTM allow secure, instant transactions, reducing the need for physical cash.
- **Agriculture:** Technological advancements have significantly increased agricultural productivity. Mechanization and modern agricultural research, coordinated by ICAR, have improved crop yields and resilience. Farming systems models and IT-enabled platforms for technology transfer have helped farmers enhance their income and economic stability.
- **Improving Productivity and Ease of Living:** Technology has greatly increased productivity and simplified daily tasks. Household appliances like vacuum cleaners and washing machines save time, while online shopping and food delivery apps enhance convenience.
- **Others:** Drones are a versatile technology with applications in disaster management, media, agriculture, construction, and defense. The Indian government's Svamitva scheme aims to create a comprehensive e-property ledger using drones to map villages. Drones also play crucial roles in agriculture, construction, and mining.

THE CHANGING NATURE OF TECHNOLOGY DEVELOPMENT AND APPLICATION AND THE RISE OF PLATFORMS

Multidisciplinary, Interdependent, and Multinational Landscape

In today's world, science, technology, and innovation are no longer siloed disciplines but are instead intricately interconnected and span across multiple nations. This transformation has made it increasingly challenging to safeguard individual technologies from competitors, whether in the military or commercial sectors. Historically, technology products were designed with specific, well-defined purposes. However, modern technologies often serve multiple functions, have diverse origins, and rely heavily on other technologies. These interdependencies involve stakeholders, users, and owners from various countries, making the research and development (R&D) process a collaborative and globally distributed effort.

The Shift from Military to Commercial Drivers

In recent decades, there has been a notable shift in the source of technological advancements. Military technologies are increasingly dependent on developments within the commercial sector. In crucial fields such as artificial intelligence, synthetic biology, and microelectronics, the journey from basic research to practical application is predominantly driven by private-sector investments targeting commercial markets. This contrasts with the past trend where technologies typically transitioned from military to commercial use. Now, commercial R&D propels much of the technology used in military applications.

The Emergence of Technology Platforms

The development, commercialization, and production of new technologies today are frequently facilitated by comprehensive systems of enabling technologies, known as platforms. These platforms consist of integrated technologies and their associated institutional and human infrastructure. They serve as foundational elements for designing, developing, producing, or utilizing specific technology applications. Platforms are characterized by their multiuse, multipurpose, and multinational nature, allowing them to support a wide range of applications on a global scale. They can be rapidly scaled, interconnected, and built upon, amplifying their impact. Examples include operating systems, telecommunications networks like 5G, the internet, genome editing technologies, and microelectronics fabrication technologies.

Platforms enable the rapid, large-scale, and cost-effective development of new technology applications by incorporating shareable technology elements. Typically developed and operated by the private sector, these platforms have become indispensable within the technology ecosystem.

Disruption of Traditional Technology Protection Methods

The rise of systems-based technologies and platforms is challenging conventional methods of protecting technology. Because these platforms are shared across numerous applications and users, traditional approaches of restricting knowledge or usage are impractical. Such restrictions could disrupt other technologies that rely on the same platforms, many of which are vital for U.S. national security and economic competitiveness. This issue affects all stages of the technology life cycle, from development through production to end-use.

THE EVOLVING GLOBAL COMPETITIVE LANDSCAPE

Shifts in the International Arena

The United States currently contends with a competitive international landscape that starkly contrasts with the environment that influenced its post-World War II competitive and research strategies, policies, and procedures.

Global Challenges to U.S. Leadership

Countries worldwide are challenging the U.S.'s longstanding dominance in fundamental research and technological innovation. They have adopted successful U.S. strategies such as establishing top-tier research and development (R&D) ecosystems, cultivating and attracting talent, and heavily investing in technology development. Given the robust R&D frameworks of these nations, it is increasingly impractical to prevent competitors from developing technologies similar to those created in the U.S. merely by restricting access or usage.

Globalization of Research and Production

The globalization of industrial research and production is driven by the increasing cross-border flow of information and people. This trend is evident as firms transform into multinational enterprises with affiliates and customers worldwide or enhance their offshore research and production capabilities. Moreover, the U.S. is no longer among a select few nations producing highly educated individuals who drive innovation in emerging technologies. Other countries now produce more STEM (science, technology, engineering, and mathematics) graduates than the U.S. and attract individuals educated and trained abroad, including those from the U.S., to apply their expertise locally.

Rise of China as a Near-Peer Competitor

The United States faces a formidable near-peer competitor in China, which has systematically pursued dominance in key technology sectors over the past two decades. China's strategies include massive investments in R&D—surpassing the U.S. in certain areas—leveraging a well-educated labor force three times the size of the U.S., and attracting global talent. Unlike the U.S., China operates under a different set of rules and worldview. The Chinese government plays a significant role in commercial technology development, often diverting or stealing research outputs and data from competitors. Foreign participation in the Chinese economy is tightly regulated and monitored, technology standards and regulations favor domestic technologies, and market conditions are manipulated to benefit Chinese companies. China acquires technology through company acquisitions, foreign-talent programs, and intellectual property theft, exploiting the U.S.'s bureaucratic responses to such actions to hinder its own innovation capabilities.

Challenges of Protecting U.S. Technological Edge

Historically, the U.S. has reacted unilaterally to external technological threats from adversaries. However, this approach is less effective in today's global R&D ecosystem and poses the risk of unintentionally hindering technological development and competitive advantage. The U.S. research community faces an increasingly complex web of policies, processes, procedures, and requirements that govern science and technology R&D. The expansion of these regulations, along with the growing number of government stakeholders exerting authority, has created a convoluted set of rules that vary significantly across federal agencies. These restrictions impede idea exchange, limit participation, and curtail international collaboration, ultimately slowing research progress and making U.S. research environments less appealing to talented individuals.

CHAPTER 8

DISCOVERIES AND INVENTIONS

Throughout the annals of history, human ingenuity has been the driving force behind countless inventions that have not only transformed our world but also shaped the very fabric of civilization. From the wheel to the internet, these inventions, whether simple or complex, have enabled us to surmount formidable challenges, enhance our quality of life, and pave the way for unprecedented progress. This article invites you to embark on a fascinating journey through time, delving into some of the most pivotal inventions in history and examining their profound impact on society.

Ancient Innovations

Our journey begins in ancient times, where early humans made groundbreaking advancements that laid the foundation for future progress. The invention of the wheel around 3500 BCE in Mesopotamia revolutionized transportation and trade, facilitating the movement of goods and people over greater distances with less effort. Similarly, the creation of written language by the Sumerians enabled the recording of information, communication across generations, and the administration of complex societies.

Classical Era Contributions

As we move into the classical era, we encounter significant contributions from ancient civilizations such as the Greeks and Romans. The Greeks' development of geometry and the early principles of engineering led to architectural marvels like the Parthenon and the aqueducts. Meanwhile, the Romans' innovations in road construction and sanitation systems set new standards for urban infrastructure, improving public health and connecting far-flung corners of the empire.

The Renaissance and Scientific Revolution

The Renaissance period heralded a revival of learning and discovery, with inventions such as the printing press by Johannes Gutenberg in the mid-15th century. This invention democratized knowledge by making books more accessible, sparking widespread literacy and the spread of ideas that fueled the Reformation and the Enlightenment. The subsequent Scientific Revolution introduced inventions like the telescope and microscope, which expanded our understanding of the universe and the microscopic world, respectively.

The Industrial Revolution

The Industrial Revolution of the 18th and 19th centuries marked a dramatic shift from agrarian economies to industrialized ones. Key inventions such as the steam engine by James Watt powered factories, locomotives, and ships, significantly boosting production and transportation. The cotton gin, invented by Eli Whitney, revolutionized the textile industry by vastly increasing the efficiency of cotton processing, while the telegraph, developed by Samuel Morse, transformed communication, enabling instant information exchange over long distances.

The Modern Era

In the 20th and 21st centuries, technological advancements have continued to reshape our world at an accelerating pace. The invention of the airplane by the Wright brothers in 1903 opened up new possibilities for global travel and commerce. The advent of computers and the internet has revolutionized every aspect of modern life, from how we work and communicate to how we entertain ourselves and access information. Innovations in medicine, such as the development of vaccines and advanced surgical techniques, have significantly improved health outcomes and increased life expectancy.

Each invention throughout history has contributed to the tapestry of human progress, addressing needs, solving problems, and creating new opportunities. These remarkable achievements reflect the boundless creativity and resilience of the human spirit. As we look to the future, the continuous evolution of technology promises to bring about even more transformative changes, further shaping the course of civilization. Join us as we explore these significant milestones and appreciate the ingenuity that has driven humanity forward.

INVENTIONS RESHAPE OUR EVERYDAY EXPERIENCES.

Inventions have the power to introduce groundbreaking technologies, generate employment opportunities, and enhance the quality of life. To help students explore this concept, we will examine the contributions of three notable inventors: Leo Wahl, Samuel F. B. Morse, and Benjamin Franklin. By comparing and contrasting their work, students will gain insight into the inventive process and its impact on society.

Leo Wahl and the Barber Industry

Leo Wahl revolutionized the barber industry with his invention of the electric hair clipper. Recognizing the limitations of existing barber tools, Wahl experimented with designs until he created the first hair clipper powered by an electromagnetic motor. This innovation significantly improved the efficiency and precision of hair cutting.

Activity:

- Examine an Advertisement: Show students an advertisement for Wahl's electric hair clipper. Allow them time to read the description and analyze the features.
- Discussion Questions: Ask students what problems they think Wahl was trying to solve based on the ad's features. Encourage them to think about how these features might have addressed issues faced by barbers.

Samuel F. B. Morse and the Telegraph

Samuel F. B. Morse, initially trained as an artist, developed the telegraph to communicate more quickly with his family across the ocean. Observing electrical sparks and their timing, Morse invented Morse code—a system of dots and dashes that could be transmitted over wires to convey messages over long distances.

Activity:

- Diagram Analysis: Present students with a diagram of Morse's telegraph device, covering the bottom half of the image initially. Ask them to study the diagram and speculate on the device's name and purpose.
- Class Survey: Conduct a survey to gather students' thoughts on the telegraph's function.
- Reveal and Reflect: Uncover the bottom half of the image and encourage students to think-pair-share about how this new information influences their understanding.
- Historical Context: Display an image of service men using the telegraph during World War II to decode Morse code. Ask students what this suggests about the practical applications of Morse's invention.

Benjamin Franklin and Bifocal Lenses

Benjamin Franklin, known for his diverse inventions, created bifocal lenses to improve his vision. In a letter to his friend George Whatley, Franklin explained how these lenses allowed him to see his food clearly while also observing the facial expressions of those around him.

Activity:

- Diagram Study: Provide students with a diagram of bifocal lenses. Have them analyze the diagram and develop explanations of how the lenses work.

- Discussion: Encourage students to discuss how Franklin's invention might have improved daily life for people with vision problems.

Inventive Thinking Exercise

Prompt students to adopt the mindset of an inventor. Focus on a common classroom object, such as a door stopper, and brainstorm ways to improve it.

Activity:

- Criteria and Constraints: Offer students criteria for success and constraints related to materials, time, and cost.
- Design and Investigation: Guide students through planning and conducting an investigation based on their design models.
- Assessment and Iteration: Assess how well their inventions meet the criteria and constraints. Provide time for them to refine their models and retest.

Reflection on Innovation

Throughout history, inventors have used their creativity to develop products that enhance our daily lives. By studying historical examples, students can be inspired to think innovatively and potentially become the inventors of tomorrow. How can these stories of past inventions ignite the spark of innovation in your young learners?

9 Technological Inventions That Have Changed the World

These groundbreaking inventions have paved the way for countless other innovations, transforming our planet and significantly impacting human history. Each has contributed to changing our environment and advancing society.

1. The Printing Press

Invented by Johannes Gutenberg in the mid-15th century, the printing press revolutionized the production of books. This innovation facilitated the widespread dissemination of ideas, particularly religious ones, and significantly boosted literacy rates and the establishment of libraries throughout Europe. The printing press played a pivotal role in transitioning from the Middle Ages to the Renaissance by making knowledge more accessible. The first major work printed was the Bible. Despite initial concerns about machines replacing jobs, the printing press birthed a robust industry of printers, booksellers, and writers.

2. The Steam Engine

The steam engine, invented by Scottish engineer James Watt in 1775, was a cornerstone of the First Industrial Revolution. It transformed transportation and machinery, shifting the economy from agriculture and trade to industrialization with increased production capacity. The steam engine led to the creation of locomotives, steamships, and early automobiles, paving the way for various combustion engines and aircraft. Its impact was profound, fostering the growth of middle classes and urban centers.

3. The Light Bulb

Although Thomas Edison is often credited with inventing the light bulb in 1880, he built upon the work of others like Humphry Davy, Matthew Evans, Warren de la Rue, and Joseph Wilson Swan. Edison's enhancements made electric lighting practical and widely available. The light bulb revolutionized daily life by extending work hours and spurring the development of electricity-generating plants and household appliances. This invention is considered one of the most significant since the discovery of fire.

4. The Telephone

Alexander Graham Bell, a Scotsman and expert in speech and hearing, patented the telephone in 1876 while attempting to improve the telegraph. The telephone revolutionized communication, enabling instant voice transmission over long distances. Early telephones required manual wire connections to establish calls, a process streamlined with the development of the telephone network. This invention marked the beginning of modern society and laid the groundwork for mobile telephony.

5. The Airplane

In 1903, the Wright brothers achieved the first powered flight with their Wright Flyer, a brief 12-second flight that laid the foundation for aeronautical engineering. Their work inspired the development of commercial aviation. Charles Lindbergh's non-stop transatlantic flight in 1927 was a milestone in aviation history. The airplane significantly boosted trade, culture, and tourism, becoming a crucial component of the global economy.

6. The Personal Computer

Personal computers have transformed how we live and work, simplifying tasks and enhancing data storage and processing. The invention of the transistor in 1947 was crucial, replacing vacuum tubes and enabling smaller, more reliable electronic devices. The Kenbak-1, created by John Blankenbaker, is considered the first personal computer. Microprocessors, developed in 1971, were another key innovation. The Xerox Alto introduced the graphical interface and mouse in 1973, while the Altair 8800 in 1975 popularized personal computing with Microsoft BASIC, developed by Bill Gates and Paul Allen.

7. The Internet

The Internet's development began with the connection of four university computers to ARPAnet in 1969. Vinton Cerf's development of the Transmission Control Protocol (TCP) in the late 1970s was crucial for sending files between computers. Tim Berners-Lee's introduction of the World Wide Web in 1991 transformed society, enabling new forms of interaction and economic growth. Telefónica's

Infovía service in 1995 popularized the Internet in Spain, bringing it into Spanish homes.

8. The Mobile Phone

The first portable mobile phone, the Motorola DynaTac 8000X, was launched in 1983 by engineer Martin Cooper. Initially, mobile phones were used solely for voice communication, but they evolved to include functions like SMS and email. This evolution paved the way for smartphones, which offer internet browsing, photography, music playback, GPS navigation, and social media connectivity. Today, mobile phones are essential in both personal and professional life.

9. Artificial Intelligence

Alan Turing, a pioneer of modern computing, is also considered the father of artificial intelligence (AI). The term "artificial intelligence" was coined in 1956, marking the presentation of the first AI program, Logic Theorist. Today, AI manifests in various forms, including chatbots, voice assistants, autonomous vehicles, real-time translators, artificial vision, ChatGPT, and the Internet of Things. AI continues to evolve, promising future applications and uses beyond current imagination, with generative AI becoming increasingly significant.

The Most Recent Discoveries

In January 2022, a remarkable discovery emerged from southeastern Australia, shedding light on an ancient rainforest that thrived between 11 to 16 million years ago during the Miocene epoch. Dubbed McGraths Flat, this site offered a treasure trove of fossils, providing an unparalleled glimpse into the intricate ecosystems of the past. Preserved within the rocks were minute details of life, from delicate spiders, down to the finest hairs on their legs, to fish with their stomachs filled with midges. The level of preservation was so exquisite that even the pores on fossilized leaves, once responsible for absorbing carbon dioxide, were discernible. Matthew McCurry, a paleontologist at the Australian

Museum Research Institute, expressed the significance, stating, "Because of the quality of preservation, we can see into these ecosystems like never before."

Meanwhile, NASA's Perseverance rover embarked on a pioneering mission in the Jezero crater on Mars, once believed to be a water-filled basin. Surprising discoveries unfolded as the rover traversed the crater, including thin purple coatings on rocks reminiscent of microbial-induced rock varnish found on Earth. Additionally, Perseverance collected 14 rock samples, a crucial step towards future missions aiming to retrieve them. In September, the rover embarked on the exploration of an ancient river delta, marking a significant milestone in our understanding of Mars's geological history.

On the Oregon coast, a centuries-old mystery was unraveled as remains of a 17th-century Spanish galleon, likely Santo Cristo de Burgos, were identified. Known as the "Beeswax Wreck" due to blocks of beeswax occasionally washing ashore, the ship's hull remnants were discovered in a sea cave near Astoria. Analysis of the timber revealed a match to hardwood used in 17th-century Asian shipbuilding, confirming its identity. In the realm of medical science, a groundbreaking achievement was made at Yale University, where scientists successfully preserved multiple pig organs, including the brain, heart, liver, and kidneys, an hour after the animals' death. This breakthrough, facilitated by a solution called OrganEx, holds promise for extending the viability of human organs for transplantation.

In the natural world, the Kingdom of Tonga witnessed a volcanic eruption of unprecedented intensity from the Hunga Tonga-Hunga Ha'apai submarine volcano. The cataclysmic event sent shockwaves around the globe and generated towering tsunami waves, prompting scientists to urgently study its peculiarities for insights into volcanic behavior. In Southeast Asia, new species of snails astounded researchers with their diminutive size, with one measuring only 0.6

millimeters in diameter. These discoveries underscored the remarkable biodiversity of cave ecosystems in the region.

Amidst these scientific endeavors, the UN's Intergovernmental Panel on Climate Change released a sobering report highlighting the imminent health risks posed by climate change. Urgent action is needed to mitigate the adverse effects on human health, including extreme heat stress, air pollution-related lung damage, and the spread of vector-borne diseases.

In a rare display of ecological resilience, a native bobcat was observed preying on Burmese python eggs in the Florida Everglades, signaling a potential shift in the balance between invasive and native species. From the depths of space to the depths of the ocean, 2022 was a year marked by extraordinary discoveries and challenges across scientific disciplines, offering glimpses into the wonders of our world and the mysteries that continue to intrigue and inspire exploration.

INDEX

J

L

M

N

O

P

40, 42, 44, 45, 46, 65, 71,
78, 83, 84, 88, 92
productivity, 12, 14, 16, 24, 25,
26, 27, 28, 29, 30, 31, 39,
43, 66, 70, 71, 72, 73, 82
prowess, 3, 26, 52

Q

quantity, 29

R

raw materials, 33, 34, 42, 45,
67
resilience, 3, 4, 10, 11, 15, 24,
72, 77, 82, 89, 96
resources, 3, 5, 9, 11, 15, 17,
18, 23, 26, 27, 33, 37, 39,
45, 46, 49, 57, 59, 61, 62,
64, 65, 67, 69, 81
revenue, 13, 17, 71
revenues, 13, 71
Revolution, 25, 26, 29, 30, 31,
33, 36, 88, 92
roads, 8, 15, 16, 17, 71

S

sales, 43, 71
schools, 17
Security, 51, 56
services, 7, 10, 12, 13, 16, 17,
24, 25, 27, 28, 29, 30, 35,
64, 65, 66, 68, 71, 72, 73,
75, 76

skills, 10, 17, 23, 24, 71, 72,
77, 81
social protection, 17
society, 8, 17, 18, 22, 23, 34,
35, 39, 49, 64, 79, 80, 87,
89, 91, 93
specialization, 26, 27
strategic, 3, 12, 13, 15, 16, 47,
49, 50, 52, 53, 54, 55, 57, 62
strong military, 47, 48, 53
supply chain, 16, 40, 42, 44
sustainability, 16, 32, 43, 65,
72
sustainable development, 17,
18, 42, 62, 67, 69
sustainable economic, 15, 43,
74, 79
system, 2, 22, 37, 51, 55, 70,
81, 90

T

Tax, 13, 71
techniques, 28, 29, 30, 69, 70,
88
technological, 13, 23, 24, 26,
27, 28, 29, 30, 48, 52, 59,
60, 66, 71, 72, 75, 76, 77,
78, 79, 80, 83, 84, 85, 88
technology, 18, 26, 28, 31, 34,
48, 57, 69, 72, 73, 75, 76,
78, 79, 80, 81, 82, 83, 84,
85, 89
territory, 3, 58, 61
Trade, 26
transformation, 22, 23, 24, 29,
38, 45, 51, 76, 82

transportation, 15, 29, 34, 42,
  43, 49, 62, 65, 67, 71, 72,
  73, 81, 87, 88, 92
transportation networks, 15, 73

U

unemployment, 5, 8
United States, 2, 3, 12, 18, 26,
  31, 41, 43, 47, 48, 49, 51,
  52, 55, 56, 57, 61, 84, 85

urbanization, 5, 25, 64, 72

V

vegetables, 37, 44

W

war, 4, 49, 53, 55, 56
workforce, 5, 30, 36, 38, 71, 72